Rescued from Hell
An Odyssey of Deception and Discovery

STEVE EVANS

Savannah, Georgia

Rescued from Hell: An Odyssey of Deception and Discovery
2012 by Steve Evans

Distributed by Healing Streams Ministry, a division of Forerunner Ministries, Inc.
  4625 Sussex Place, Savannah, GA 31405
  Email: info@healingstreamsusa.org
  Website: www.healingstreamsusa.org

Published by Forerunner Ministries, Inc.
ISBN-13: 978-0615597935
ISBN-10: 0615597939

Edited by Anne-Marie Evans.

Unless otherwise indicated, all Scripture quotations are from The Holy Bible, English Standard Version® (ESV®), copyright © 2001 by Crossway, a publishing ministry of Good News Publishers. Used by permission. All rights reserved.

Scripture quotations marked (WEB) are from The World English Bible (public domain).

Cover and interior design by Forerunner Publishing, Savannah, Georgia. Cover image used with permission from Microsoft.

Printed in the United States of America by CreateSpace.

TABLE OF CONTENTS

PART TWO: THE RETURN

Preface

In the weeks and months that followed my conversion to Christianity in 1982, I had a great desire to share what my lost years had been like and to tell the story of how Jesus rescued me out of them. In the beginning it was surely a lot about my own need because it felt so good to be able to express the craziness and horror of those years *in the past tense*—and find in return some soothing measures of sympathy and understanding. That believers were inspired and encouraged and that unbelievers occasionally came to faith added immeasurably to the wonder of having a story like mine to tell.

I began to notice, however, that the more I shared my testimony with all of its bizarre and wildly insane aspects, the more I felt my *otherness* from others, and that was not what I needed! I desperately wanted to recover a sure sense of my common humanity—to *feel* human at last. Yet, sharing my testimony made me feel like a freak all over again because I never once came across another testimony remotely like my own nor could I avoid colliding with the emotional wreckage I was still wading through, pain that no one I met had a good remedy for or prior experience with mending.

People would tell me to trust the Lord, encourage me to give it to God and slap me on the back, saying how great it was that the Lord had delivered me. All of that was true, of course, but I had no idea *how to do it* with the internal damage that was still screaming for attention. Jesus rescued me from hell! Yet, I had been dropped back on earth with a ton of still scary stuff that was clinging to me like glue.

There followed then a long season of seeking inner healing: every conference I could go to, every book I could read, every prayer line I could find. All that grace gives as ways of bringing our hearts to God, I started applying in earnest. My journey through those years has brought me to a place where I am no longer in conscious touch with debilitating emotional damage. There may still be pockets of resistance, some even with surprising depths, but in terms of the day-to-day I am living way above and beyond my past, not because I am trying to push it down, but because I have pulled it all up—everything I could find. I have vigorously thought about it, prayed about it, given it to God piece by remembered piece in so many effective ways. I have actually become glad and grateful for all the experiences that I went through—a seemingly impossible turn of events!

My heart's desire is that *this time around* my story will not be about me (though I am on every page), but about telling truth in a way that will help people out there, especially the ones who feel that their own path has been so tortured, so strange, so completely inexplicable to others that they feel isolated and estranged from the common run of humanity. Take heart if that describes you—for in the early days of my recovery I often challenged God saying (not politely), "Are you sure you can do this? Have You ever brought somebody back from this extremity of insanity and bondage? Will I ever feel human again?" How brash and belligerent! Yet I was desperate to believe that I wasn't stuck with being broken and freakish *for the whole of this life*—that God could indeed pull off that part of the rescue, too. Perhaps, however, your interest is not for your own healing but for gaining insight and understanding that will help you minister to others—I definitely had you in mind as well! The text is quite literally a primer on how to lead someone out of intense emotional and spiritual darkness by tracing the outlines of how Jesus did it for me.

I hope that you will enjoy taking this strange journey with me and that the Lord Himself will intercept us just as He did those unsuspecting disciples on the road to Emmaus, bringing liberating words of resurrection across their horizon. May these words enlighten or enliven you to see Him striding the heights beyond even those boundaries of fear and hope which may encompass your own life.

PART ONE:
THE DESCENT

*From the devil's perspective this is a story
that was never supposed to be told.
From my perspective it is a story
that should never have happened.*

CHAPTER 1

THE NIGHT OF TERROR

"All I have to do is get home tonight, take these pills and it will be all over. Death is the only way out!" The night bus carrying me home seemed to take forever. As we rumbled through the flat Carolina farmland my thoughts tumbled over the crazy landscape of the past two years—my failed "spiritual journey." I was more lost now than when that dazzling encounter with god got me going. How could I have failed so miserably to rise to the occasion, especially when so much was at stake?

With bitterness born of fear I reproached myself over and over for having missed out on connecting with my god. *I was lost, irretrievably lost to god.* But, boy oh boy, had I connected with myself. I had discovered repeatedly how shallow and vain, how cowardly and conceited, I really was. How bound by shyness and fears. How utterly unable to live with natural ease. How thoroughly fouled I was—a motor that never caught fire from the sparks. I must have been dreaming to think *I* could pull it off.

A veil had been pulled back, a veil that had kept me in a dreamy cloud of naïve egotism all my growing years. Now, at twenty-three, I saw myself as I truly was: soul-less and sin-filled. Less than two years before in the presence of that light, thrilled by a divine awakening, I was drawn into revelations of a universal life meant to be shared with everyone. Now I just wanted to run and hide. That same light which showed me my god had eventually shown me too much of myself. There was no way out of the failed person I discovered myself to be and no way back to the happier (but unenlightened!) person I had been before that fateful day of revelation.

No wonder that just three weeks ago, my inner quest to unite with my god had been shattered by the experience of my soul leaving my body. At the time it was happening I knew *in my bones* that my soul was disgusted with me. Just as I was now. Everything in me that had the hope of becoming good or decent took wings and flew away. The crazy thing was that I had never before been aware of *having* a soul, but from the moment it began to depart, the awful reality of losing it was undeniable. I was transfixed in horror—this was no Faustian legend, this was *my* life—yet there seemed to be nothing I could do to rescue myself. The next day I went to my psychologist, the hated "Rock," the name I secretly gave him due to his technique of never initiating conversation, only trying to force me, through his stony silence, to speak. I never let him see so much as a glimpse of the real me.

Now, however, it was either turn myself in to the psychiatrists or head up to the Canadian northwest and hide out from humanity in hopes of not damaging anyone else with what I had become. A man without a soul is a danger to the world and (thank God) there was nothing in me yet that wanted to see harm come to others. "The Rock" put me on Meyer Ward, Duke Hospital's psychiatric unit in Durham, North Carolina. This was right at the time when I should have been graduating. After two weeks of endless tests and interminable inner torment (paranoia, self-hatred, foul thoughts) I was released. Evidently, some of the best shrinks in the world could do nothing for me. I was totally unchanged and completely un-helped, even though I had at last spilled the beans and given them everything I had been hiding away from "the Rock" *ad nauseum*.

The Duke doctors gave me drugs and sent me to a halfway house in town. The message was clear: *For me there could be no rescue.* The doctors were well-intentioned and well-informed, but they didn't have a clue how to reach me or free me. They all too obviously gave no credence to the spiritual realities I had encountered and treated them as if they were delusions. I on the other hand could look upon them in no other way than that those moments of divine encounter were the most *vitally real* moments of my life. If those moments were delusions or illusions as these doctors implied, then what was the rest of my life? They had no answer for that.

I desperately needed answers from someone. I needed someone to guide me through these spiritual realities, to show me how to make sense of what I had experienced—not to disparage it as if there was no substance to the spiritual side of life, or as if it could have no legitimate claim upon us. These scientists of the mind were practical atheists (whatever their Saturday or Sunday morning convictions may have been). They were blind guides where these spiritual realities were concerned, powerless to help one like me, caught in the grip of what Kierkegaard described as "fear and trembling" and "the sickness unto death." So I sneaked out of the halfway house my first night there. What was the point in staying? Besides it was run by a bully who clearly loved to lord it over the broken ones under his authority. I had a major aversion to bullies. I also had money enough and time to spare at the downtown bus terminal, so I hired a taxi to take me to an all night drug store. That's where I got the sleeping pills. I had no idea how many I might need so I bought two over-the-counter boxes.

When the bus pulled into my hometown around four or five in the morning, my resolve remained unwavering: Death was the only way out. I found a taxi still operating (luck was with me!) which dropped me off at my parents' house. All was dark and silent. My parents were asleep, not expecting me to be coming home from Durham. Quietly, I let myself into my room at the other end of the ranch style house. I don't remember how long I might have thought about it before I opened the first pack of sleeping pills and took them all. I don't think it was very long, but some of the details of this evening are vague. Others are seared into my memory.

Shortly after taking the pills a strange thing began to happen. Something shifted in me and I was flooded with hope. Perhaps the chemical influence temporarily broke the grip of the depressing thoughts I had been having. I don't know. I only know that to my deranged way of thinking, this moment now held the possibility of the transformation I had been seeking. The next thing is hard to admit, but it seemed to me that if I was to experience a kind of rebirth back into life, I needed to be entirely natural, as natural as I had been the first time around. That's right—I stripped off all of my clothes. I then walked outdoors fully nude in the direction of the rising sun. A brand new day was dawning—that mere fact seemed saturated with significance and supernatural potential. Alas, those sweet dreams were not to be! After only a few brief moments this gossamer sense of impending glory dissipated like a morning mist and I was left shivering, naked and exposed—exposed once again as a fool and a fraud.

I hastily returned to my room and, filled afresh with shame and contempt, lay down on my bed to die. By now I could feel the weight of the sleeping pills taking over. My eyelids had become heavy. I made no effort to resist the downward spiral. This was what I wanted, what I needed—the Big Sleep. To close my eyes and *never* awaken. To never have to be me ever again. Even if I was to be nothing at all that was still a huge plus in my eyes. I was not looking for Nirvana, much less the Christian idea of heaven. I was looking for complete non-existence and fully expected to find it. Just when I thought I was almost there, it all went unbelievably and horribly wrong.

I am well aware that I cannot take you into what happened next, nor would I wish to if I could. I was seventeen years into

my Christian life before I was healed of this one experience—
and that was almost twenty-seven years after the event. What
happened was this: Up from the hidden depths, seemingly
from the bowels of the earth, an invisible army of unspeakably
foul beings began to penetrate my mind and lay claim to my
body. Nothing I had ever thought *possible* in this life prepared
me for the sheer terror of feeling, sensing and hearing these
demonic entities scrabbling all over me.

Their insistent message projected into my mind was shocking and already being partially realized within me—they had
come to feed upon me and torment me. Forever. I realized with
horror that no one who ever knew me, in learning of my death,
would know this is how I ended. No, not *ended*. Once I actually
died no amount of screaming or resisting could change one iota
of the torture they intended. *It would never end!* With all the
strength remaining in my physical body I powered up and out
of that hellish entanglement.

Rising from the bed, I staggered into the bathroom to splash
water in my face and try to awaken further. I remember staring
deep into my eyes in the bathroom mirror in desperation and
fear, as if I could somehow summon up something from within
myself that could give answer to this horrible predicament. *Get
a grip! Think! Do something quick!* I thought death would be the
way out, but it was a trap, a sadistic nightmare that was waiting for me with gleeful malevolence on the other side of the
bathroom wall.

It was then that god showed up. The divine being that had
come into my off-campus farm house at Duke one and a half
years earlier now reappeared. Then it had been bathed in
shimmering light, filled with promise. Now it simply was
there. *More real than the floor and walls.* More real than me. I
could sense it with every fiber of my being, but I couldn't see it.
Yet, its presence was in this moment more complete than any of
the encounters I had had with it since its first appearance. I
knew full well its past displeasure with me and shrank inward-

ly at realizing that it knew also how ignobly I had failed once again to find the way to rise into its higher life.

Just as I feared, my god began reproaching me for the willful weakness, cowardice and inhibition that kept me from releasing myself to his calling. My whole life began to pass in review as I was held transfixed by the unwanted visions. I was shown everything about my life in relation to this god: what I had been given, what was expected, what I failed to do. I saw so clearly my sin as that of holding back and fully agreed within myself that it was a terrible sin, *unforgivable*.

According to the revelation I had received, the fate of the universal consciousness I had been made part of hung in the balance, so I had not only failed myself and this god, but I had failed everyone connected to me. I could not argue with the judgment that came next. I was pronounced guilty and sentenced to the damnation of eternal separation from god and from anything resembling life. I would forever be in the self-made hell of a consciousness that was meant to awaken (and bring many into awakening) but was now doomed to collapsing upon itself like the "black holes" formed by imploding stars.

Nothing could change this irreversible and final decree. There was no possibility of repentance, forgiveness, or mercy. I could not even think of those concepts. Besides, the truth was that I had failed many times over in the attempt to unite with this god and become an agent of transformation. I was totally in agreement with the judgment and the sentence. I *deserved* damnation. My guilt was unarguable, indefensible. I was now a lost soul furiously rejected by my god for reasons I completely accepted. I held myself in bitter contempt—just as god did. Hell was the only possible end for one like me. What would have been the point of pleading for further chances? I had proven myself incapable of changing, unworthy of sustaining.

Eventually, the god departed, taking out of me everything that seemed like life and withdrawing all trace of hope, *even the possibility of ever having hope.* I knew that I would never again experience anything that seemed like a good, natural, wholesome or "human" emotion (and didn't for the ten years this demented mindset prevailed). All that was left inside of me was rage, ruin, terror, self-hatred and abject despair. I staggered, naked, out of the bathroom, cried out and fell to the floor. Just before losing consciousness, I was aware that my father heard me from the other end of the house, found me, and was calling the hospital. Then all went dark. It was the Big Sleep at last, only instead of being my dream of sweet nothingness, it was a stark raving nightmare from which I was fully convinced that I would never awaken.

CHAPTER 2

DUKE AND DARKNESS

What Went Wrong?

How did this terrifying calamity come about? What is the path by which a person descends into such depths of interior destruction and despair? Was it inevitable? Did it have to turn out this way? Where did the wrong turns happen that threw my life so disastrously off course? I have to say that for many years my young life seemed to be going up and up, a steady stream of accomplishments filled with many privileges. Ending in this way—eternally damned and sentenced to hell—was not something I could have imagined!

Right up to my college years, my inner storyline was filled with bright hope. A rosy picture of my life usually played on the screen of my imagination. Now after the space of many years I can see that there were a few dark undercurrents, which I either chose not to see or pushed down and failed to act against. In the absence of a wise and understanding spiritual guide who can help you carry your unwanted parts to God and show you how to release them, I had no better plan than to ignore and repress them. I suspect this is most folks' fallback position and it was admirably expressed in the film "Gone with the Wind" by Scarlett O'Hara who chose to avoid "going crazy today" by thinking about her troubles "tomorrow." We all know of course that *that* tomorrow never comes, except when it is too late for well-considered action, though it is far easier to recognize the danger of delay when viewing someone else's life. For me the enlightenment I needed came slowly and painfully—and not nearly in time to spare me from wrecking a perfectly good beginning.

One early unpleasant trait was a tendency to sulk for which I was often punished by being barred from outdoor play. I grew out of it, but later when doing drugs I fell back into this same pattern of futile brooding. Other undercurrents were pride and egotism running rampant inside me. These I never grew out of—they only got worse with time as my ability to gain approval and achievements increased. I began to daydream endlessly of even greater glories. Ironically, I was painfully shy and taking great pains to try to conceal it. Looking back I can see that somewhere along the way I lost connection to my true, natural self and never noticed its passing. Worst of all, I entered into a fantasy life where girls were concerned. It was benign and innocent enough at first—I imagined myself their hero—but by high school years it had become a full blown pornographic obsession. Also by high school I had developed an aversion to one of my family members and I did nothing to rein in my secret antipathy.

What was my answer to these egregious moral failings that I was accumulating? I simply plastered them over with a smile! My outward life was drawing such positive reviews that it never dawned on me that I was becoming truly reprehensible *in my inner life*. Nor did it seem strange that one of my deepest fears during high school was that while walking the darkened hallways at night I would turn a corner and run into, not Satan, or even a demon, but Jesus Christ. This thought spooked me to no end, but it never occurred to me that it was a very strange thought for a baptized Christian to have about his professed

Lord and Savior. Oh, the foolish self-absorption of youth! That we imagine our own life somehow sets the standard for normal. The very One I needed most to meet was the One I wanted most to avoid—and, as I have said, I thought nothing strange about it. The one I really didn't need to meet at all, I ran head-first into at college.

Do Bee, Do Bee, Do

It was at Duke that my wheels came off the track. Not at first of course. There was so much positive momentum coming out of high school that I simply flowed in the strength of better habits for most of the first two years after my awestruck arrival in 1967. The truth is that part of me was and always has been a "Do Bee." Do Bees (for those who don't remember the TV program, *Romper Room*) were those happy, praise-worthy children who do the right thing. As a Christian I now realize that there is a blessing that God gives to each of us whenever we do the right thing, at the right time, in the right way. He is assuredly a Rewarder and though the reward comes anonymously and is often rather low-keyed (a nice warm feeling for instance) it still offers good natured Do Bee's reason enough for buzzing about happily.

There is however another system of rewards out there. It works by playing upon the natural affirmation that people give us for doing well, and twists it into the sweet, intoxicating nectar of reaping praise. Imbibe too much of that heady liquor and you will find yourself working for approval and acceptance, rather than the quiet contentment of a task well done. The former feeds ego, the latter the soul. How can God compete with that? Not even drug trips can be compared to the addictive allure of ego trips! I was hooked and as long as I targeted classwork, I stayed focused on the professors' approval. Eventually, however, the desire for the approval of friends and leaders in the burgeoning student movement won out. I cut the lifeline that kept me tethered to the only legitimate reason for being in college—getting an education—and began to drift into dangerous areas, areas with treacherous predators hidden in the depths.

By the spring of 1968 the mood on campus had turned decidedly towards national politics. Attitudes began to grow strident, then ugly. There was talk against the war, outrage over civil rights issues and great interest in the presidential election campaign. As a reporter for the Duke Chronicle, I skittered around the edge of the political debate: covering a George Wallace rally in Durham, the campus sit-in when Martin Luther King was assassinated and later Nixon's inauguration in Washington. My actual assignment, however, was to be an entertainment writer which I loved because it got me into all kinds of events for free, but which I hated because I *knew* that I knew nothing about being an art and theater critic. People were bound to catch on. It never occurred to me to ask for an assignment I could actually do.

Wooed by the Spirit of the Age

In the meantime I was being radicalized by association: The editors of the school paper who I held in awe, the professors I most revered, and the national leaders I respected all came from the side of the political spectrum I had once been taught to disparage. To my surprise I found myself fully admiring their compassion, their concern for social justice and their intellectual flair in expressing their views. By contrast, it seemed to me that too many right wing leaders at the time failed these tests. These liberal-minded men were urbane, sophisticated, *in the know*—everything I now wanted to be. I simply could not find the way to substantiate my innate conservatism without appearing foolishly ill-informed, so I surrendered it without much of a struggle.

Now, in my later years I can see that I had apparently embraced a mindset (conservatism) without understanding the underlying rationale sufficiently to stand up against the assault taking place upon it. I love the saying often attributed to Winston Churchill: "Show me a young Conservative and I'll show you someone with no heart. Show me an old Liberal and I'll show you someone with no brains."[1] If that is right, then by degrees I began to "lose my mind" as my heart for radical politics increased, but that was nothing compared to what came later when I "blew my mind" on drugs.

My real love, however, was the world of ideas opening to me at university, not always in the classroom. Literature, psychology, philosophy, anything in the intellectual history of the West—these were my great interests. A class on Russia launched me into searching out the writings of Karl Marx, the Russian anarchists, and other social revolutionaries. They had an intriguing aura about them (as opponents of authoritarian oppression) that cast further glows over my new political heroes. Somehow I got on to Freud. Then I devoured Carl Jung and Herman Hesse, both of whom blended the Western scientific world and Eastern mysticism in a way that really gripped my curiosity and moved me, unknowingly in an occult direction. This led me to embrace much of the New Age thinking, which was making wide inroads on campuses at the time. Tarot and "cosmic consciousness" would come later. The wooing stage of occult penetration is more benign.

I also had classes in the religion department which carried me further afield: In one class I learned that the Bible was written by men, not God, and therefore could claim no particular authority over me. In another class I was taught that all religions are basically the same and therefore Christianity could claim no special revelation for me—just what I was hoping to

---

[1] The phrase originated with Francois Guisot (1787-1874): "Not to be a republican at twenty is proof of want of heart; to be one at thirty is proof of want of head." Wiki-quote, *List of Misquotations* (accessed June 29, 2012).

hear. These were days in the wake of the "God is dead" theology, which sprang up from this same religion department. That too was fine with me. In my whole time at Duke, I don't think I ever went into the magnificent chapel even once. I certainly never attended a church service anywhere that I can remember—though I had rarely missed a Sunday during my teen years in Kinston, North Carolina. It was as if my early Christian upbringing had never taken place.

All of this drifting towards darkness came with time. I hasten to add that there was nothing in what I was reading that *of any inherent necessity* drew me into drugs and the occult. Another person could have read the same books and kept a sane perspective. But I didn't. Something in me, or about me, kept tugging at me to wander beyond the pale of a sensible and rational world view. I did nothing to stop the downward trend. I actually thought I was rising higher, at last. How was this possible? The Bible reveals that one of the undercurrents in everyone's life is the negative attraction coming from generational patterns of the past. What our forebears did or didn't do doesn't force us to stumble, but according to scripture, it can lay a snare across our path.

Although I knew little of it at the time, three of my near ancestors were involved in the occult: one with Christian Science, a Christian cult; another with Dianetics (renamed Scientology), a non-Christian cult; the third with the Masons, a pseudo-Christian cult. Please don't misunderstand me in this: In no way am I blaming them for my own foolishness. The choices I made were my mistakes alone. I love these family members (though none are still alive) and I am very sure they had no idea they were transgressing into the enemy's camp—any more than I did. They would have been shocked to be told that their own spiritual searches were misguided, horrified to think that they might have loosed something hurtful upon the generations that followed.

There is one who *knew*, however, and he is a legalist who never forgets, who loves working under the radar, and whose greatest trick is to get us to disbelieve in the reality of his existence and of his arsenal of powers. You may not share the Biblical perspective on generational patterns, but it shines a light for me into the mystery of why spiritual darkness had such an allure, even though no one took me by the hand and showed me the forbidden territory. Nevertheless, there was a drawing, a beckoning, that seemed *natural*—a familiar path, so to speak, for one in my family line to tread.

In fact as early as the spring of freshman year, I was investigating the medieval alchemists. These were rascals and charlatans in one view (the correct one), proto scientists by another, who believed that there was a way to turn base chemicals into gold and who managed to make a nice living at the courts of credulous kings. Goethe's Faust is their most famous exemplar in literature. Best case scenario? They were promulgating a religion of transformation, whereby the baser elements of human personality could be raised to display something far more sublime. Like those benighted medievals, I was credulous enough to think there might be something to it. Deep down I knew that there wasn't, but I began to pretend to myself that there was.

This was partly a way of rebelling against my father, the scientist and chemist, whose conservative views I was beginning to renounce. But there was a hook in it. In *The Heart of Darkness*, my favorite novel from those days, Joseph Conrad wrote about "the fascination of the abomination" that attracted the doomed Kurtz to go over to the dark side of African life. Something like that came over me where medieval alchemy was concerned. By the time summer arrived I had even invented a fanciful "religion of darkness" by inverting the words of St. John's Prologue. It was a shameless ploy to attract the attention of women by acting like a free thinker. Free thinker? I did not have the remotest idea to whose thoughts I was actually becoming enslaved! For this blasphemy God graciously forgave me through

23

saving me, but that liberation was to come much later, after so many bitter tears, and long after true spiritual darkness had removed the smirk from my face.

It was during spring semester sophomore year that I began questioning traditional Christian sexual morality in earnest. By then I had a foreign student girlfriend, the cultural winds were blowing in from Haight-Ashbury in San Francisco and Bob Dylan had us all singing about how the times were changing. I can only state that it was a genuine struggle—I needed to become convinced in my conscience. Sad to say, but when push comes to shove (the push of moral training vs. the shove of actual temptation), many men go with the thoughts coming from what's below the belt, rather than what's above the neck. I proved to be no different.

Sigmund Freud was excellent for showing how the process works whereby rational thought is subverted by suppressed desire. The trouble was that his theories seemed to justify allowing sexual desire to lead the way into life and love, rather than (in Christian terms) crucifying it as need be in order to enter the life of covenantal love that God intends. Behind all this inner obfuscation is the one the old Quakers called "The Reasoner," nick-named after his deft ability to make the wrong thing seem right and the right thing seem wrong. If temptation was not plausible and the desired object unseemly, the enemy would gain few converts. As it is, his lies seem eminently reasonable to the one giving them ear. The word for this is very apt: rationalization, the process of becoming convinced by telling yourself rational-*lies*. Perhaps you have taken the course. I majored in it at the university!

Yet how can I explain to you the perversity of our inner contradictions? We are apparently quite capable of thinking one way and behaving just the opposite without ever calling ourselves to account. Blaise Pascal observed that we are a mystery even to ourselves (*Pensée* 131). This was certainly true of me. All the while this genuine moral debate was going on within me about sex before marriage, I was stoking the unholy fires of a pornographic addiction that I had been secretly pursuing since my teenage years. I never once stopped to consider the moral implications! I cringed, felt enormous shame, lived in constant terror of exposure—and kept going. Small wonder my conscience at last became convinced, or rather silenced, by the "new morality." Sex, drugs and rock and roll steamrolled right over my final faint objections to abandoning the wisdom of two thousand years of Judeo-Christian moral teaching.

Prayer? What's That?

Why, you may ask, did I not pray for help, or strength, or guidance? The answer is simple: It just didn't occur to me. I never had been one to pray in the morning or at bedtime, never said grace at meals, never even called upon the Lord in moments of doubt or fear, trouble or adversity. I never considered that God was actually Someone you might want to talk to. It was silent on His end. I assumed that was the way it was meant to be, so I quite naturally kept it that way on my end. And yet I had been raised to think of myself as a Christian. *Christians pray!*

As far as I can honestly recall there were only two prayers I ever made during the Duke years. The first was during my junior year. I remember standing on the circle at main campus where we waited for busses. I looked up to heaven and said (something very much like this): "God, I know You are out there somewhere. You were known in the past to the Jews and the early Christians. You don't seem to be in Israel or in churches now. You must have moved on. I'm going to spend my life trying to find You so I can bring You back to others—or die trying. I don't care if it kills me, I have to find You!" Twelve years later, *after* the Rescue, I realized that God had actually answered that prayer; He answered it alright, but in the strangest of ways.

I am sure you can see the conceit of that foolish, though earnest, prayer. God doesn't need anyone to find Him—He's not the one who is lost! But can you hear the heart yearning? God did. That at least was a part of me that was real. Even so, this was *the* moment when I fully, self-consciously, closed the door on Christianity as a possible avenue to God. I was well aware that my next move would be to open the door to "mind-expanding" drugs as a way of trying to find a higher spiritual life. How little did I realize that if you shut the Jewish-Christian God out, there is only one other alternative out there—the one scripture calls *the god of this world*. He is the father of lies, the initiator of all false religions, the impersonator of the One True God. All over the world he goes by many names. The Rolling Stones were singing out a warning in those days about having "Sympathy for the Devil"—that if we didn't figure out who he was before it was too late, he would lay our soul "to waste." I should have listened, but I thought it was merely rock and roll poetry, not rock hard reality. The other prayer I saw answered very quickly, though it's best I save that one for later.

Throughout the fall of 1970, after that prayer at the circle, I began experimenting with drugs. Beginning with marijuana and some serious laugh attacks, I tried hash, then LSD. As "advertised" whole new vistas opened before me at first: I saw indescribable beauty in the most ordinary things (eggs in a frying pan, for example); actually heard harmonies for the first time in my life (hysterically, between a Beatles record and the whining of our plumbing); encountered the reality of an almost sacred life existing in nature (the astonishing Otherness and Aliveness even of trees). I began to "break out of the box" in other ways as well. A Jewish friend and I got high one beautiful fall day and painted my prized VW bug with all the colors of the rainbow. She painted a Star of David on the roof—I loved the decorative touch. That star-spangled bug became a hippie icon on campus. I eventually sold it to a German divinity student who worked with me at the Chronicle, but while it was mine, I gloried in it.

These sightings of the distant shore encouraged me to believe that my voyage of discovery was indeed sailing in the right direction. Then the rougher waters came. Psychedelic trips that began full of promise heaved my mind way off course. Wild imaginings, paranoia, mind-bending possible versions of reality began to capsize my sense of what was real. While watching *2001: A Space Odyssey* stoned, I became convinced, absolutely convinced, that I was looking through the theater screen at primates of the remote past *in real time*—and that they were looking directly back at me. It took considerable effort to fight down the urge to try walking through the theater screen—what a spectacle that would have made! On another occasion trees began speaking to me. I didn't know what they were saying, but they *were* vying for my attention! I couldn't get a handle on it and I wouldn't stop trying. Why couldn't I master these trips? Everyone else seemed to be having a good time, while I alone was cracking up, losing my mind and becoming a drag on everyone else. Eventually, things came to a head, though not in any way I could have predicted.

CHAPTER 3

THE GOD OF THIS WORLD

An Unsolicited Visitation

The pivotal event occurred after Christmas break senior year. I had been home trying to make sense of things and playing George Harrison's *All Things Must Pass* album endlessly. That didn't help, but neither did the hometown surroundings. High school dreams and high school friends seemed light years in the past. I had tried to connect with some of them: Those who were still devoted to the old patterns seemed like foreigners; but even the ones who were into drugs, seemed to be on a different wavelength from me. I couldn't relate to anyone or feel at ease with them. What was wrong with me? The part of the drug culture I had entered held up the hippie ideal of a person completely at ease (caricatured in comics as Robert Crumb's "Mr. Natural"): laid back, earthy, one with nature and at peace with the universe. I was anything but that! I was breaking down, but not breaking through.

So it was in abject dejection that I returned in January of 1970 to the small off-campus farm house I shared with my roommate since sophomore year, Bobby R. I really loved this guy—we traveled all over the East coast, usually taking his purebred Irish setter, Sean Sol Hampstead d'Aberdeen, with us everywhere we went. We covered the map while engaging in wide-ranging academic debates which I always seemed to lose. It was immensely maddening at times. I once shot back: "Here I am struggling to figure things out and you seem to have known everything the right way from birth!" The humbling was good for me—I just didn't appreciate the taste of it at the time.

At the moment though Bobby had not yet returned from break. I had the house all to myself, which was not a very pleasant way for me to have it, considering my frame of mind. I was thoroughly ill at ease within myself. My early years had been so full of promise, yet everywhere I looked I saw my life circling downwards: Relationships and romances were a bust, I was clearly a dilettante intellectually and dreams of making a name for myself through some glorious career were completely shattered. I wasn't really considering suicide, not in any practical way, though the thought was looming in the background. It just seemed that the life I had been pursuing was ending and I had nothing with which to replace it. I desperately wanted a chance to start over. This sounds so melodramatic, but I promise you I was feeling exactly as if my life were spiraling down like a flushing toilet.

What came next was totally unexpected and unsolicited. I was not doing drugs at the time, had not done any drugs since going home for Christmas several weeks before, so this experience was not chemically induced. I was lying in bed in the late afternoon, awake and thoroughly depressed, when to my complete astonishment, a glowing, bright light began to appear across the room where wall met ceiling. It was shimmering and lustrous, brilliant but not blinding. It appeared to be somewhat oval in shape, approximately two feet wide, with no definite boundaries. Like a cloud, it simply suffused a kind of radiance, strongest in the center. Did I say it was a light? It was infinitely more than light—it was life, *the* life I had been searching for ever since that impassioned prayer at the main campus circle! This light had *being*. Instinctively, I sensed that it was god.

Then without any audible sounds, communication began. Words quietly emerged within my mind, which began explaining the revelation. At this late date I can't recall word for word what was projected into my mind, but the general meaning remains as clear now as it did that late winter afternoon. I was in the presence of god, *the* god of this universe, the god who *is* this universe. My mind was being merged with his—my consciousness was being awakened and united to that universal consciousness which so many poets and wise men had known. I recalled, rather was made to hear phrases like "the inner light," "the eternal now," "the life force." There was no message of Christian morality, only a heightened awareness that this eternal being united all things at their deepest level in love and harmony—perfect oneness—whether they were conscious of it or not. I was graced with experiencing the life that had been within me and around me all along.

This god—the universe itself in realized self-awareness—had sought me and called me, knowing that I had been searching to find it. I had to have been willing to cast off the tradition bound shell of my former life to enter into this discovery. By some untaught reflex I "shrugged off" my past life and it seemed to slip even further away from me like a snake shedding its skin. I felt entirely reborn—not through forgiveness, but through enlightenment. A childlike wonder arose and with it came a sense of that natural grace for living which had so long eluded me. The highest point of this calling was to raise me, not only for the sake of my own personal transformation to higher life, but for the sake of also reaching others so that a new age could dawn for all of mankind.

This calling was both gift and responsibility: The fate of all that my consciousness now touched somehow hung in the balance to rise or fall with me. It was imperative that I find the path of releasing myself into the flow of this universal spirit. I was made aware that youth all over the planet were undergoing awakenings similar to this one. I also became hazily aware of past lives: dying upon the beach at Normandy, a romance during the Victorian period and hints of things further back. I never dwelt upon these "memories" and certainly didn't try to "recover" others, but they were at once unnerving and intriguing at the same time.

Like everything else in the presence of that light, these experiences seemed real enough in the moment—far more real than the whole of my previous life. How long did the time last? It seemed as if time had been suspended, for so much was compressed into the enrapt awareness of revelation—every sense heighted beyond the customary level and my thoughts shooting about like bottle rockets in response to what I was being shown. In real time it may have only been a mere handful of seconds. I simply don't know.

In the Wake of Awakening

Then, just as quickly and inexplicably as it had appeared, it was gone. I was shaken, exhilarated, undone, turned inside out, put back together, rolled into one and then poured out on the silent shore—but of what coastland? I thought life would never be the same again. No, I knew life *could* never be the same again! I had crossed over, been brought over actually, to the other side of *not knowing* about this god. I now "knew" god and was "known" by him: Where do you go from here? You certainly can't go back! I was high with expectation and near giddy with delight. How easily I could have gone through all of life and missed this! How easily I could have been left sleeping in the dark of an unawakened consciousness, dreaming the egotistic and self-created dreams that accompany it. This was the ultimate adventure! Now a whole new world lay before me to explore, the world of a universe in the pangs of rebirth—that much was certain. The part I was to play in the coming transformation—well, that was by no means clear. That uncertainty scared me a bit, but I foolishly thought myself equal to the challenge.

As cliché as it now sounds, this period of the late '60s truly seemed to be for me and many in my generation the "dawning of the Age of Aquarius"—a time when humanity would finally come into its own. Before "cosmic consciousness" ever gained notoriety as a phrase, it was first an experience, one that was widely shared and which carried unquestioned authority—*as an experience.* I don't recall ever using those terms much myself, but they sufficiently express the inchoate ideas that were gripping me. Everywhere I turned these same ideas were now leaping out at me through the lyrics of rock songs, the writings of *our* poets and assorted spiritual guides, and most significantly, through the inward communication now established as a pathway for my listening mind. Everything in creation was by definition a part of this universal consciousness and could be used as a means of communication with me. I was all eyes and ears.

Even so, it came as a shock to me to discover how difficult it was to communicate to anyone else what I had experienced—what I now *knew* to be true—not just of my life, but of all life. It also shocked me to discover how little capacity I had for braving the quizzical looks and skeptical resistance I often encountered. Where was my courage? Where was that heroic nature that was supposed to be part of my newer, deeper self? I was caving in and retreating like a frightened tortoise into my comfortable shell of shyness. Only it wasn't comfortable any more. It had been exposed, along with so much else, as being part of the *old* me—the *false* me—not the new me. *Oh god! I'm trapped in my shell, stuck in the cocoon all over again and can't get out! Show me the way!*

These weren't prayers exactly. I never really set about to pray to my god, but my thoughts were definitely going off in that direction. Looking back from a more experienced perspective, I am afraid that in those days I was unwittingly praying to myself! I had considerable lifetime training in looking to myself to find the ability to solve school problems, beat sports opponents and win awards. A deeply ingrained inner reflex kept me looking to myself to be my own savior, even where my relationship with my god was concerned. And yet how badly I wanted that relationship!

I was trying desperately throughout this period to reunite with both the sense of communion and the flow of communication that came whenever he deigned to draw near. Those times of unheralded encounter were never under my control and never very long in duration. They were, however, the focal point of my striving, reinforced a feeling of specialness in being granted them and always renewed hope about the supernatural possibilities for my life, if only I could succeed in letting go of the "death-grip" I placed upon myself. This proved impossible for me to do. It literally became my un-doing.

I didn't go down without a fight, however. Against all the reasons my parents or others could muster, I decided to drop out of Duke with just one semester left. My reason was that I needed to devote myself more fully to this spiritual quest. Nothing else mattered! When my roommate (wisely) declined to tread with me on my journey, I moved out, or perhaps he asked me to move out—many of the details are fuzzy. That same drug daze which so often accompanies marijuana and hashish abuse not only puts the practitioner into a fog at the time, but it casts a haze over memory as well. In fact I can just barely remember times when it seemed like whole chunks of knowledge about different subjects, especially math and the sciences broke off and drifted away, never to return. While under the influence of what we had smoked, it seemed hilarious; now I wish I had it back.

What I could never get back was the ease of letting go that I had experienced, an ease where everything in me gave way to the inrush of that first heightened encounter with god. I began reading more of overtly New Age literature and dug into the music which seemed to carry the heaviest "spiritual" payload (the Moody Blues, Steve Miller Band, the Incredible String Band, etc.). Oh, and naturally I did more drugs for which I can't recall paying; however, I must have had to pay at least on a few occasions. There were of course many friends who shared their stash freely and who seemed to "have it together" far better than myself. I looked to two in particular for guidance, listening attentively to anything they had to say, hoping to grasp the secret of how to live like the liberated, free-spirited hippie I was hell-bent on becoming.

One of these friends spoke into my life a word that has remained with me to this day. We were at a local restaurant famous for its honey fried chicken; trying to be funny, I pointed out a lady with an overly painted face and made some deprecating remark to my friend. He rebuked me saying that in his experience such a woman might very well be covering her face to try to hide a broken heart. *Had I thought of that?* Deeply ashamed I knew he was right to rebuke me and probably right about the woman. I was shown a window into a world of sympathy and understanding that lay within my friend's heart. I mention this to give color to the portrait of what we thought of as our hippie "tribe." We were not all drug-crazed hedonists and egotists; or we were not just that, at least not in the beginning. Friends of lower quality came along later, after a disastrous trip abroad, after I gave up all practical hope of finding a way to force my sinking ship to right itself.

Holland and Other Destinations

Europe was a natural destination. I had fallen in love with Paris on a study trip to France during the summer following my junior year in high school, so much in love that I cried when our return flight lifted off, grieving the thought that I might never return. Two years later I was back, having recruited some college friends to go with me for a summer of archaeology in Winchester, England. We bought an Austin Mini in London and managed to cram all four of us in, including our bags. With two weeks to go before the start of the dig, we boarded a car ferry, crossed over to the Continent and headed straight for Paris! None of my friends dared drive in the teeming Parisian traffic, so I had the car, if not the streets, to myself. For me it was heaven—"Toad's Wild Ride" all throughout the City of Light. Once settled in at the dig, a better love came along in the form of a girl from the Channel Islands. That summer of '68 raised my young life to heights never reached through my recent drug trips, yet I failed to make that connection on my return flight two years later. My whole agenda had changed.

Hopes of seeing my first love again seemed reason enough to return to Europe, along with visiting a Dutch girlfriend in Holland, but my real purpose lay in wanting to connect with my ancestral roots. I was desperate to get my spiritual journey on track and I thought something about being in the land of my ancestors would hold the key. I was wrong, so very wrong! Europe had no keys for me to find, only bars and locks.

The single worst drug trip of my inglorious career, perhaps one of the top ten acid crashes of the whole misguided era, awaited me in The Hague, Holland. I was working in the receiving department for a satellite manufacturing concern on the North Sea. Our janitor, Klaus, served tea to us with enormous, sea-toughened hands Durer would have loved to engrave. I can see them still. The bus to work carried me past incredible exotic sights: vast fields of tulips in full bloom, a breath-taking array of brilliant colors, soaking in the northern sun. I had never seen anything like it. The ancient burgher town itself was beautiful, interlaced with canals and dignified by cathedrals. On market day some of the most delectable cheeses in the world could be bought for mere pennies on the dollar.

We lived in cramped quarters above a bar owned by a local politician. The bar was fittingly named *De Bonte Koe* ("The

Good Cow"). Indeed, life was good. So was the Heineken. But I was restless—increasingly warped and wrapped up by my obsessive search for release from my self-created prison. This all goes to show how little I knew then that getting free within (even aided by the Lord) is akin to Chinese handcuffs. I know now that the more you fight against what is binding you, the stronger its hold upon you grows. This becomes force multiplied when it is yourself you are fighting against! True freedom operates *by grace* through faith. That's God's way. My way out of any bind? By now this should come as no surprise. Someone I knew offered me acid, so on a day off with no one around to interfere, I took the whole hit. Then the debacle began.

By now the border between fantasy and reality, strong in most folks, had become severely compromised within my own mind. The sturdy world of everyday, mundane reality—the world of *things*—which tethers sane people to a common sense view of life, had become an ever-shifting collage of entry points for the world of *spirit* that both transcends and infuses all things. My encounter with god had taught me that what is not seen is far more real than what is. The unarguable truth was that I had never before that encounter *seen* god; I had only seen the world of things which obscured him—yet his was the most real *being* I had ever encountered. With the gift of enlightenment, that same world of things had now become his avenue for revealing the astonishing depths of universal life which had been there all along. As the acid kicked in I opened to that world that lies beyond material sight and began to float upwards into heightened awareness of it.

At first the sights and sounds were heavenly! Colors were suffused with light. Distant echoes were woven into song and music seemed to fill the air. I became convinced that I was hearing angels beyond the walls and ceiling of our flat—more so, I felt that it was intended that I hear them. They seemed to be summoning me upwards through the spirit into fuller view and conversation, but I couldn't find release from my doubts and inhibitions (*Suppose this wasn't real, after all? Suppose I was going crazy?*). I faulted myself severely for these weaknesses. When I sensed the trip heading for a crash, I went outdoors in hopes that a change of location would give me a fresh chance to connect. I hated and feared it when things got this strange, but I was determined to ride it out, never dreaming that just around the next bend, Bizarre was coming at me like freight train!

I have always loved to watch the play of light upon the water, so naturally I headed in the water's direction. Soon I found myself in a grassy area under some trees beside the still canal, but I could not find a corresponding place of rest inside myself. By now the natural beauty around me was provoking a profound desperation to be at one with it. How it came into my mind to take off my clothes and enter the canal is easy to answer—I was wide open to *any* vagrant thought wandering through my mind. There was no watchman at the wall, no keeper of the gate. I had been replaced by the one I would later disparagingly call "Stevie Wonder." I came to hate his foolishness, for he caused me no end of mortification! The reason for stripping down was simple enough to understand: Get back to nature. That would solve everything! Even while writing this, I still cringe at the memory of how easily I was made a fool by the one who mastered me in those days. I was clueless, emptyheaded: a true "Stevie Wonder."

On this late July afternoon, that unguarded side of myself began swimming through the canal. The downtown streets of The Hague were filled with solid, sensible Dutch citizens who were now noticing me, waving for their friends to have a look and gaping at the naked madman doing the American crawl in their canal. Eventually I grew tired, so I angled towards a wooden house boat and tried to pull myself up on deck. A woman on board suddenly appeared with a broom and, very sensibly, beat me back into the water; I resorted to plan B and swam towards a bridge, climbing upon it. Two officers were waiting there to make the catch. Their combined grip was very strong, but rising from nowhere, I reached within myself and found the power to easily throw them off. Perhaps you have heard that the insane have such powers? Take it from me as one who knows, they do. I was in the grip of *sheer blind panic*—I could have run all the way back to France.

As it happened I ran into the city square that lay on the near side of the bridge. Wondering what to do next, with all the shoppers in a flurry around me and the policemen closing in, much to my surprise, a man pulled up in a small car and asked *in English*, "Do you want to get away from these people?" That's just what I wanted to do! I shouted, "Yes!" and hopped in, but when he asked where I wanted to go, I had no idea. Just then I noticed that the late afternoon sun was going down. That couldn't be allowed to happen—the "dying" sun seemed like too terrible an omen. "Drive!" I yelled, "In the direction of the setting sun!" And away we went, driver fully clothed, Stevie Wonder naked and soaking wet.

I could hardly believe my luck, though in typical fashion, it didn't last very long. We hurtled around a corner or two, catching glimpses of the sun as we went, until we came upon a police road block and were stopped. I had been caught! I was taken to jail for the night, where I was treated with stitches for the nasty wound I had incurred when climbing barefoot into the canal. To this day I don't know the identity of my benefactor, whose car became my brief means of escape. I don't even know if he honestly tried to make a clean getaway or intentionally drove me straight to the police; though I suspect it was the latter. I didn't fault him for it—I was too amazed that he had shown up when he did. It was the closest I had ever come to being rescued inside one of my living nightmares.

There was, however, a lot of well-deserved fault-finding coming my way, though not from the police. Strangely—but it was all strange—the police seemed to be satisfied that I simply had a bad acid trip and was now safely restored to my right mind (such as that was). Perhaps they considered that having a bad trip was punishment enough; after all, Holland had been home to the Enlightenment. For whatever reason, no one pressed charges. They gave me my clothes and released me the next day.

There was quite a stir in the local paper of course, intensified by the fact that the politician we were renting from happened to be running for mayor at the time. I was told that my antics dampened his chances for election and that he was quite put out with me. I truly felt bad about that, but as a hippie I had a low opinion of politicians anyway and figured it was no great loss to the world. My Dutch girlfriend was not impressed with me either, but still stood with me. However, I betrayed her faith in me even further. I could not bear the shame or deal with the defeat, so I made some pathetic excuses and left on the first freighter I could find that would ferry me across the Channel to Winchester, England. "Miraculously," a friend there, having received my desperate wire, had hired me for another season of archaeology. I felt like a cat tossed out in drenching downpour, but at least I was landing on my feet.

I won't go much into my second season at "the dig" because it was mainly a healing and fairly uneventful time in terms of further disasters with drugs, which mostly brought me back into the more healthy patterns of my previous summer there. Seems like I'm glossing over something, right? Ok, now that I think about it, there was one excruciatingly bad evening of weed. I was sharing a joint, possibly two, on the town green with some companions who decided we should visit a tavern while still high. It seemed like a good idea at the time—you would think I would have learned some semblance of a lesson. But no, as soon as we got inside, I had a spooky feeling of no longer being in merry *modern* England. Except for the style of their clothing, the serving girl, the barman and everyone at table seemed to be acting exactly like they would have been back in the Elizabethan era. They also seemed entirely alive to the thrill of it, an eerie form of group consciousness of which all seemed a part.

It was a timeless scene, doubtlessly played out in real time over and over through the centuries, filled with rough humor, ready wit and rollicking good times. But for me it was an all too real window into actual Elizabethan *time*. Here we go again. I was convinced that I was being invited to enter into a transcendent reality—shared by all of them—at a level of engagement that was way beyond my ordinary powers. I totally freaked out. My companions had pity on me and walked me to their flat. The entire walk was accompanied by a bitingly cold headwind, blasting against us—as if to say, "Coward, why did you leave? Turn back." That I couldn't do. I couldn't bring myself to go back to the bar and make another attempt at overcoming my cursed inhibitions. Transcendence would have to wait. There was always hope for tomorrow, at least there still was in those days.

Uninvited by me, the words of a James Taylor song began playing in my mind about how "a cold wind" would turn anyone around. I knew I was failing another test. I trudged on, a condemned man. This marked the first time that I had the distinct feeling my god was angry with me, menacingly angry, and it certainly would not be the last. My friend played "Abbey Road" to soothe me, yet *in my mind* god twisted all the lyrics into direct maledictions against me. I was terrified. My heart felt as cold in my chest as the wind outside. Paranoia had arrived to stay.

It wasn't paranoia, however, that gripped me a month or so later when my return flight brought me to Kennedy Airport in New York. No, it was legitimate panic! Seeing the drug-sniffing dogs and the long lines at customs, I suddenly remembered I had a small bag of marijuana in my backpack. Why had that thought not occurred to me sooner? I was torn between wanting to solve the riddle of my imbecility and finding a solution to the looming disaster. The truth is, as well as I can remember it, that I really had little desire to light one up since that perfectly awful time in England that I just described. This was old weed that had probably languished there for some time, unnoticed, untouched and unwanted in the bottom of my pack. Forgotten by me, but about to be discovered by *the Man* if I didn't come up with a plan and fast!

Old unwanted weed can get you busted as quickly as the good stuff: "But officer, it's *just* a bag of dried out twigs and seeds!" I couldn't see that going over well. Fortunately for me, there is a God and for some reason of His own, He covered my foolishness *that time.* I saw a trash can (*fantastic!*), the kind with a lid and a flap (*amazing!*). What idiot—God bless them—put that hiding place inside the customs area? As calmly and nonchalantly as I could, I sidled over to it and disposed of the contraband. To this day I wish I could see a digital replay of that moment. I am sure I looked anything but innocent. After all, I was bearded with long hair, wild in the eyes, dressed every bit the hippie and disheveled from having slept outdoors in Luxembourg the night before. And this was before profiling became politically incorrect! Yet no one noticed. I walked out a free man, rescued once again by an unsought quirk of fate. All I could think to do was thank my lucky stars and like Jimi Hendrix pause to kiss the sky! *Thank You Father. I didn't know You to thank You properly then. You were my secret Rescuer.*

Stateside and States of Mind

Back home in the states, hanging out in Durham, North Carolina, with my usual group of friends from Duke, I discovered that life seemed to be taking a nasty turn for others as well. A dear friend, who seemed so much wiser and kinder than the rest of us, had died during the summer in a car accident in the Appalachians—his van had gone over a cliff. Another member of "our tribe" and his girlfriend had been abducted at gun point while hitchhiking through Florida and were put through unimaginable hell until they escaped. This was the fall of 1971 and society was in turmoil due to the cultural revolution at home and the Vietnam war abroad. I was barely aware of it. There were much darker things going on in the world beyond our tribal boundaries, but I wasn't reading the headlines any longer: My world was shrinking.

In dropping out of school I had also been dropping out of vital connection with so much else in life without realizing it. Gone was my early activism. Gone were the former interests in causes, the political arena, even art and literature. These had slipped away, leaving no trace. This is typical of those who "drop out." The other side of this descent, of course, is what you drop into. Life is an uncharted land lying wide open before us (uncharted for those that don't read the Bible). We need to know, however, that the landscape has a hole in it—a deep, dark *terrifying* hole. Some call it "the pits." Take the wrong steps and you stumble. Stumble enough and you start to tumble. As for me, I was falling fast.

I made a quick trip out west to Kentucky, hitchhiking my way through the mountains, so I guess neither of my friends' fates had left a lingering caution. Kentucky didn't prove to be the "easy chair" I had hoped it would be, so it was on to Nashville for a visit to my older brother—the family member I had developed an aversion to during my high school years. Unaided by anything we did to patch up, the drug culture had produced a miracle—we were fast friends again! It happened in this way: I was in DC in January, 1969, covering the Nixon inauguration, or maybe it was later in the spring when I went up as part of an anti-war protest; that part is hazy. What is crystal clear though is this: I wandered onto the Mall just south of the White House with my knapsack and notebook. From out of nowhere came mounted police throwing tear gas into the milling crowd of students. Many of us ran for higher ground—the Washington Monument—to escape the police and the noxious fumes. At full trot I practically ran straight into none other than

43

my infamous older brother. His first words won me over: "Well, I'll be a g-d d*#*#d, son of a b*#*h! Would you like a joint?" I didn't take him up on the offer—the police were too close and I was still just on the edge of "the movement," but from that point on we were "black sheep" together.

Now, several years later, I was truly feeling like an outcast, so it was only natural that I chose to camp out with my brother, though that meant hanging out with him *and* his first wife, a proto-feminist and sadly one who would have given the honorable side to the feminist movement a bad name had anyone made the connection. One night, very early into my visit, my brother and I went out to see a Bruce Lee movie and do a little male bonding. We came home entirely sober at the appropriate time. You would have thought we had been out molesting children and ripping the throats out of babies for all the moral indignation heaped upon us for having watched a picture of such alleged violence.

I guess it's okay to be violent with *words*. Just don't *look* upon violence in movies. It wasn't her fault of course—she had had a terrible upbringing at the hands of a man. In those days practically no one was getting free of their childhood trauma. Even so, we were all trying whatever we could find that *might* work. For her, releasing anger at the men in front of her somehow helped soothe the anguish caused by the one behind the scenes, the one from her earlier years. Understanding her anguish only compounded our frustration. Compassion can be so unsatisfying at times, since it leaves you no one to pick on. We pitied her, but she was still scary to live with.

Eventually, I headed back to Durham and the comfort of old friends, old friends which included the familiar set of hallucinogenic drugs—marijuana, hashish and acid. It was another exercise in futility, like my sister-in-law and her anger, but with this pointless pattern I was the one who couldn't connect the dots: drug trip... bad trip... crash landing... slow to no recovery. *Wow, man, that was a bummer. Got some more weed?* What was hooking me was not the "high"—I was no longer getting high, wasn't sure that I ever had. What hooked me was *not* getting high. How crazy does that sound? Yet, it all made perfect sense to me.

The one overriding issue of my life was union with god and the personal transformation that would come through that, if I could only crack the code. Remember the first prayer I ever made—the one at the Duke circle? *I want to find You or die trying.* I thought all good hippies were seeking God same as me. That's how naïve I was—and how shallowly I probed the inner life of my friends. They were out for a good time and a good feeling, nothing less and nothing more. Not me. I was in it to bag the Big Game—God.

In my mind drugs had become the only thing that could open me to those spiritual encounters which held the possibility of presence, *release* and growth. Something seemed to be holding me back, though, resisting my every effort to give myself in total surrender to my god—a surrender my god increasingly demanded, not without threats and displays of temper. My only thought was that it was me—my cursed weaknesses, cowardice and inhibitions. Years later I learned that all along it had been my God, the One True God, the Christian God that I had so thoroughly renounced, who was secretly and mercifully thwarting my every effort to unite with an enemy I had mistaken for Him. My obstacle wasn't something in me; it was Someone beyond me. However, I knew none of this at the time, yet despite my lack of knowledge, I managed unwittingly to get off a prayer in *His* direction.

Remember that I told you that there was a second prayer? This one occurred during this same fall season in Durham right after a perfectly awful drug trip had left me crushed and broken. Something about the drug "high" was causing me to see myself from a perspective I had long evaded—honest self-reflection. Playing Frank Zappa while high was taking a sledge hammer to my vaunted self-opinion—but without any grace or mercy to cushion the blow. Time and again a self-centered layer was exposed amidst the rubble: This time I had seen how selfishly I was living. I cried out, "God if you can somehow put me back together, please let me do things in life *to help other people*, even if I have to work as a janitor." A few weeks later I scored a part time job I desperately needed—cleaning businesses at night. At the time I failed to thank Anyone for the answered prayer; years later of course I could see the Lord's humor as well as His Hand in that particular job. Unfortunately, the way I kept putting myself back together only ensured that I would have more crash endings to horrifying drug trips.

Going Down, Downer, Downest

We are at last closing in on the time that I introduced you to at the beginning of this book. All that is left to bring you up to that moment of attempted suicide is to provide a bit more background to some of the events I salted into that chapter as flashbacks. Once fall crossed over to winter, it seemed wise to finish what I had started at Duke four years earlier by seeking to enroll for spring semester and get the diploma. My parents must have cherished a hope that this would right my sinking ship for they agreed to finance my plan without any special pleading on my part. I'm sure that they didn't have any real idea how to help me and wished they could. I felt the same way, but whenever they tried to speak with me about their concerns, I put my walls up and turned my hearing down. I wasn't receptive to their wisdom or to the ideas of anyone over thirty for that matter, but I was wide open to suggestion if it came from someone my age.

There was a phrase I had read by one of our authors—a spokesman for the counterculture—that haunted me. It went something like this: "What happens when 'tune in, turn on, drop out' becomes 'freak out, mess up, crawl back'?" I was very afraid that I was about to find out and didn't relish the idea of crawling through the rest of my life. Sure enough, the dean of students who remembered me from my glory days during freshman year laughed out loud when he saw me among the entering transfers. *Crawl.* I could barely hold my own with the classwork. *Crawl.* My old friends were growing tired of all my drama, so I had to look for new friends. *Crawl.* One was a heroin addict in a dilapidated house where I rented a room. Junkies were the lowest of the low—no one respected them; yet even he would lord it over me and I let him. *Crawl. Crawl.*

Then came Easter week and all of my confusion about what that holiday meant suddenly became apparent to me. I knew that it had something to do with Jesus Christ, but I wasn't exactly sure what. By this time I no longer thought of myself as a Christian—that had died out with the shedding of my previous life when I had encountered what I considered to be a *real* god, not the one in books. Still I had been in church regularly, including Sunday school, youth group and even baptismal preparation as a teen. It bothered me that I didn't know what the big deal was about Easter, so *for the first time ever* I asked questions about something I didn't know, but *knew* that I should have known. I was rewarded with the information that Jesus died, but rose from the grave. He came out of the tomb. *Wow. I need some of that!* I lay down in my bed on Easter day and began fervently hoping it would happen for me. It didn't occur to me to go to a church, call a pastor, or to pray. There even was a "hippie priest" on campus that I knew; he got high. Ironically, I was intimidated by him, so I never thought to give him a call. Some kind of resurrection would come to me anyway. It just had to! But it didn't.

During this final semester—perhaps it was at my parents' request—I began seeing the psychiatrist I secretly called "the Rock." Remember how I hated his method of staring me down and that I wasn't about to give him any juicy morsels? The strange truth is that I *voluntarily* showed up for all my appointments like clockwork, why I don't know. I gained nothing from those meetings except an embarrassed rage over having to endure them. However, the thing that convinced me that I needed to "turn myself in" to the nefarious "Rock" was, as I mentioned earlier, the experience of losing my soul. In Christian terms and in actual fact, I believe now that such an experience could only be followed immediately by death. We are *living souls* so long as we have the breath of life in us, even if we feel our existence to be far from the land of the living.

The trouble is I had read too much German romantic literature. I was particularly fascinated by the Faust legend, had even cycled across England to see Christopher Marlowe's *Doctor Faustus* performed at Stratford on Avon. Well, I cycled there and it happened to be playing, but I just knew that it was *meant to be*. Anyway, Faust is the power hungry alchemist who sells his soul to the devil in exchange for entering the "holy mysteries," tapping into supernatural powers and reaping some of God's glory for himself along the way. The story really gripped me, perhaps you can see why. Little did I realize that I had *given* my soul away, when I could have actually cashed it in for some spiritual "loot" such as Dr. Faustus acquired *by bargaining*. Then, too, Goethe's Faust managed to get his soul back by the end of the book—he had a great author writing for him—mine got away. I simply cannot describe it to you. You will have to stretch your imagination around the next corner, then book a flight into the land of madness. Believe me, you don't want to know. I was there. It happened—it *had* to happen given the depths of depravity into which I had sunk. All that soul means for us in that higher, nobler sense, rose up in distaste within me and gently drifted away. I couldn't blame my soul for that; I wanted to leave me too.

My first thoughts, upon awakening the next day to soul-less living, were all about leaving. I had heard that there was a lot of wilderness in the northwestern tracts of Canada. Perhaps, I should go there? I could live like a hermit and never be a threat to anyone. I was convinced that not having a soul made me dangerous (it did, but mainly to me, not other people). If I had a scrap of moral courage or decency left I would get on a bus and disappear into the deep woods forever. For a brief while I wrestled with the decision: I rummaged around inside of me, but couldn't find that scrap. It was then that I made an un-scheduled visit to "the Rock." I could only imagine his secret surprise (nothing ever showed on the stone wall that held his eyes), when the "dry hole" —me!—that he had been sitting be-side in silence, which before had only burbled surface sludge, suddenly became a gusher.

Scientists of the Mind

"The Rock" knew just what to do and wasted no time. With my permission, or at least my acquiescence, he had me imme-diately placed in Meyer Ward, the psychiatric unit at Duke Hospital, which is a pretty *far out* place to be: not the Canadian northwest, not even remotely close to daily life in your hometown either. So, at least you were safe from me. So was I—while I remained there under lock and key and careful ob-servation. I was also relieved at first to be in the hands of the experts. Finally, someone would know what to do with me, because I sure didn't.

These professionals had to be the cream of the psychiatric crop: They had the degrees, the years of training, the clinical experience, the hallowed Duke name. Surely they had seen cas-es like mine before, would consult their collective wisdom and pull the rabbit I needed out of a hat—or at least pull me out of the rabbit hole I had fallen into. With Christianity dead for me, these scientists of the mind were the last priesthood standing: secular gurus of the unconscious. Sadly, they couldn't help me, either. Even though I reverted back to my Do Bee mode, be-came perfectly compliant to all their requests and eagerly par-ticipated in all their tests, I was clearly a nut they couldn't crack. They didn't have a hammer big enough. No one did, or so I thought.

Don't think I'm not aware of the pun by the way. At one level (the one I was on at the time) "going crazy" is terrifying; on another, insanity is absurd, even comical. As one who knows madness *from the inside,* I believe that it's my privilege to take the second path, now that I can. God knows I spent enough years running down the twisted corridors of my mind screaming in agony. The hangman may not have a right to revel in gallows' humor, but the condemned certainly does. If the rope breaks, he'll be the first to laugh.

At the time, though, I couldn't find anything to break the grim reality of my ruined life. I looked at the walls and saw pictures of Jesus: Jesus as radical revolutionary, as hippie priest, as flower child, as Protestant saint, as Catholic martyr. No explanation was given and I didn't know who to choose as the "real" Jesus. Yet, in some strange way it was searching *me* out. Those penetrating eyes didn't help my fragile mood! Fellowship, however, should have helped. After all, misery loves company—at least that's what people say, though you couldn't prove it by me. There were other kids on the ward who were close to my age and who had also crash-landed from drugs, but they were mostly local high school students who we customarily denigrated as "townies." Oddly, I noted a strange conflict within me whenever I was around them: I felt superior to them due to my college years and status and yet inferior since they seemed, as broken as they were, to be far more in touch with life. They seemed to relate easily and warmly to each other, bonding together under the duress of life on the ward. How I envied them that!

I had no idea how to join in with them, even though they kept extending an open invitation. With all the time that has passed since then I can barely visualize them, but my heart goes out to them still—I have met and worked with others like them since; however, at that time I didn't want them to see *me,* not the real me—even I couldn't stand *that* sight. One of my top ten operating principles was "don't let anyone find you out." I began shying away from them. Soon, I was stonewalling everyone, even the doctors, hiding behind an ever-hardening shell. I had no idea how to end my self-imposed isolation, but there indeed existed a hammer big enough to break down most of my walls. When it finally crushed me with full force, I found myself tasting the sweet meat of human fellowship in the most unlikely of places with some of the strangest people I have ever met. That would be at Cherry, but to get there, we have to take leave of Duke by way of a slight detour.

The day finally came for the doctors at Meyer Ward to scratch their heads one last time, load me up with medications to take, and send me down the road, literally, to a halfway house in town. Did they think it would help, or had they given up? I don't know. It was evident, however, that at least one nurse saw me as a lost cause: She was giving me the Rhorschach ink blot test, designed to get at the interior landscape by having the patient describe what the abstract images suggest to his/her imagination. In full blown Do Bee mode I gladly rose to this test. Here was something I could actually do! In fact I thought I was excelling at it—waxing eloquent with unhindered abandonment—until I caught a glimpse of the undisguised expression stealing over her countenance. She was not impressed; quite the opposite—the contempt, even disgust, was unmistakable. That was when I realized it is one thing to despise yourself; another thing altogether if others join you in that assessment.

The doctor's assessment of me was something that came out later, much later—and only then by accident. It happened some time during the middle of my ten years "in hell" (which you will learn about soon enough), during a flu type visit to my family practitioner in Morehead City, North Carolina. For some reason he was called out of the room and in his haste my case history was left wide open on his desk. Naturally, I became curious. I had just enough time to read the main paragraph of the Duke report before he returned. Their diagnosis was paranoid schizophrenia. I could handle that. That was actually pretty mild compared to what I really was experiencing.

What stung most was the offhand observation, "He smells." I took offense with that nasty little zinger. Being labeled a paranoid schizophrenic was okay; truth be told, it seemed to fit the bill well enough from the outside, but *not from the inside*—they were way off there. Their diagnosis also had the added advantage of dignifying my insanity with an appropriately heavy label. I would have hated it if they had thought I was a mere neurotic.

Honestly, I *was* paranoid—somebody was definitely out to get me and had; I *was* a divided soul (schizophrenia comes from Greek roots which literally mean "split mind"); and I had been ripped clean in two, forever separated from the person I had once been. The truth was also far stranger than that. Shakespeare's Hamlet admonishes his friend, "There are more things in heaven and earth, Horatio, than are dreamt of in your philosophy." Even nightmare can become reality in the world of spirit. My doctor's sudden return interrupted my reveries. He handled the situation well, very consoling, even encouraging: He had a friend in college who was schizophrenic. It happens sometimes to that age group, my age group. His friend recovered. I can't recall, but I hope I was happy for his friend.

I was genuinely grateful for my doctor's openness with me. It was far more by way of sympathy and explanation than I had ever received at Duke. Those doctors simply released me and had me ferried me over to a Durham halfway house—all without a word of understanding passing from their minds into mine, beyond instructions for taking my pills. I remember that my parents came up, helped me settle in, wished me well, then returned to Kinston, North Carolina, for the night.

This was all so *humiliating!* Jacked up on legal chemicals I was a zombie, hardly able to put two thoughts together in time to make a third: *What'd you say? Huh? I dunno.* Shrug, shrug, cringe, cringe. Presumably, I was meant to start my life over under the operating principle that half a mind is better than a crazy mind. The halfway house was supposed to help me get the rest of the way back to normal. Admittedly, I didn't give it a fair chance. That first night the guy in charge invited me to play billiards, and when I—the druggie misfit—began to beat him at his chosen game, the grins came off and something bearlike and bullying showed through. As soon as bedtime came, I sneaked out of there. This was home therapy, not house arrest—the real lockup was only a day away, but I had no idea I was leaping from a frying pan into the fire.

This is where you joined me on this journey, remember? We opened with the bus ride home which came after fleeing the halfway house bully and hailing a taxi to pick up some sleeping pills from an all night drug store in order to seek refuge in the Big Sleep. With me now? What I didn't take time to tell you in that first chapter was the way the one true God was reaching out to me. The whole way to the drug store and back to the bus station, my taxi driver was telling me *his* whole life. It seemed that he had family members with all kinds of problems who were depending on him. To add to his troubles he was overweight and aging and had some major health issues of his own, but he was obviously hanging in there, doing the right thing. The contrast with my life and with what I was planning to do couldn't have been more apparent. I somehow knew that "the universe" was sending me a message. Despite the deep shame that rose within me, I refused to listen. My mind, or what was left of it, was made up—I was hell-bent on pulling the curtain down. The play was over—I had no part left to play that felt like *play*. It was time to head for the exit.

Consider re-reading that first chapter now as a memory refresher, before going on to what I awakened into once the Big Sleep became the Night of Terror.

CHAPTER 4

THE YEARS IN HELL

Cherry Hospital

My time "in hell" is going to be hard to describe to you for several reasons. First of all, for the sake of keeping with the *experienced* reality of those days, I have to write as if my hell were the real hell. Obviously, it was not—but I was absolutely convinced at the time that it was. The story of the next ten years will not make any sense to you if you don't get this point and it is apparently not an easy point to get. I felt the anguish of this difficulty very keenly once through something a Christian psychologist said to me after a year of weekly one hour sessions: "Most people say that their lives *were* hell; you were actually *in* hell." I shouted out, "That's what I have been trying *all year long* to tell you!" If you want to take this journey all the way with me, you will need to "listen" better than that trained professional.

Another problem is that the fog of so much demonic activity crowding through my thoughts and emotions makes it hard for me to remember things as clearly as I would like. You might ask why I would even want to remember how bad it was? That's easy—*for the sake of healing*, so that I can become fully whole. The scriptures show us that whatever is brought to the light becomes transformed: Light *always* overcomes darkness. Bringing things merely to the light of remembrance, I grant you, is often tormenting. But bringing trauma to the Light of Christ becomes liberating—once you learn how to fully release it to Him. I have often joked that I was the Grand Central Station for demons in our area and that they were sending messages out to their friends, "You're having a slow day with your host? Come over here, Steve is wide open. The party's always on!" Even as I write these words genuine humor is flowing through me in remembrance of those days. That's what I call a good recovery. Still, there are a lot of muddled up things in my memory.

A final difficulty may come for you in reading so many superlatives. I love Ernest Hemingway as much as any *aficionado* of terse description, but terseness is not my forte. Besides, Hemingway wasn't writing about the supernatural. He was intent on bringing things down to earth. He wanted his readers to taste it, to see it. When I read him, I'm right where he takes me—I even want to reach for a cigarette and a glass of wine and I haven't smoked or drank in ten years! However, where I want to take you is way beyond Papa H's here and now into the timeless, trackless wastes of eternity below. This was ordinary, common sense reality shattered beyond recognition— normal life rendered FUBAR on a cosmic scale.

Not only that but superlatives are the order of the day, whenever the *super*natural manifests. I can appreciate St. Paul's predicament—he was taken up to heaven and shown things that were "unlawful" to express. I, on the other hand, was taken down, and merely shown things that are *unseemly to describe,* though I assure you, I wish they had also been "unlawful" to experience. Just know that I am not some hyperbolic teenage author for whom a word like *awesome* is suitable for describing a fresh slice of pizza; at the time of this writing I am sixty-two years old and in the full enjoyment of a balanced life. I am now, thankfully, a fairly ordinary guy. These past events, however, were anything but ordinary—they were entirely off the chain!

The Snake Pit

When I awakened in what I came to think of as the "snake pit," my life was decidedly *on* "the chain"—busted and locked up, inside and out. From that time to the present, I have very vague memories of what happened during the days that immediately followed my "night of terror" suicide attempt described in the first chapter. Though I barely remember that night, doubtlessly I was rushed to the local hospital, had my stomach pumped and was assessed by the doctors. I seem to recall it being explained to me that, because of my suicide attempt, state law required I be transferred to Cherry Hospital, the regional mental facility in the next town over.

I couldn't have cared less. Nothing mattered now—nothing except the overwhelming judgment that was fully upon me. The doctors of course didn't know it, *couldn't* know it, but from my demented perspective, I had actually died in what they called my suicide "attempt." I was *in* hell—that was a fact, the one great overriding FACT of this continued existence. Yet, I was also convinced that no one *in this hell with me* would ever believe or acknowledge the reality of what I was experiencing. Were they even alive? I honestly didn't believe that they were—not here, not with me. I believed that they lived on in some other universe still united to the god who had abandoned me. I could have screamed incessantly and would have, only somehow I also *knew* that hell would be exquisitely responsive to me, never in a good way. That was part of the torture—you could easily make conditions in hell worse, but you could never make them better.

Coming back to full consciousness in the "snake pit" at Cherry Hospital didn't help my first impressions of hell one bit. I believe I was in the "pit" a week, maybe two, but it may only have been a few days. It seemed to be a holding tank of sorts, where the powers in charge kept us while they ran their tests, formed their treatment plans and made up their minds where to place us. The pit was crawling with insanity. It saturated the air. It writhed upon every face. It was laced through every garbled conversation with the dozen or so others incarcerated with me. This was the summer of 1972 and "mainstreaming" the mentally ill had not yet been adopted as public policy. Instead, all of us from the criminally insane to the "retarded" (our word at the time), to those wacked-out on drugs like myself were crowded into the locked wards.

In the throes of the drug epidemic and the cultural upheaval brought in by the '60s, business was booming at Cherry. Eventually, a new policy would release many to the streets, but for the moment I was shoulder to shoulder with a lot of really eerie people. We were simmering—each one of us—in a witch's brew of inner torment. We couldn't help but to bubble over, spilling craziness onto one another, filling the air with the noxious fumes of our incoherent mutterings. We milled about the main room like caged animals. I remember Procol Harum's *A Whiter Shade of Pale* was playing frequently, causing me acute discomfort. The title described how I felt; I also imagine it described how I appeared.

The truth is that I didn't care how I looked, or sounded. During the only conference at Cherry that I can remember with the psychiatrists, I set all decorum aside and said over and over to them, "I'm doomed. *Doomed!*" Actually, I wasn't just saying those words, I was *pleading* them, trying to "push" their meaning—the reality that gripped me—into the minds of the professionals across the intervening table, just in case there was anything they could do. The effort would prove futile. Indeed, it was evident that they could neither see nor believe in the spiritual reality that had laid me to waste. In my mind these were second-stringers anyway—custodians, not healers. I had been worked over, to no avail, by the real experts at Duke, so I gave up all effort. This was the one and only time that I tried to open up to *anyone* about the interminable nightmare of the hell I was experiencing. *In hell there could be no rescue from hell.* From that point on I was back to stonewalling the shrinks and refraining from talking about my inner reality with anyone. What was the point?

There were unrelenting conditions to hell. One, the most terrible of all, was abject hopelessness. In Dante's *Inferno* the gates of hell are inscribed, "Abandon all hope ye who enter here." That is so true! Where there is life, there is always *some* hope to cling to, no matter how slender it might be, no matter how foolish. Even in my tormented last days, I had the hope that suicide would make things better. Foolish? Yes. Slender? Certainly! But it was hope nevertheless. Now there was absolutely NO hope. No hope that god would return to me and repeal his anger. No hope that the judgment against me could be reversed. No hope that I was anything but already dead and in hell, damned and soulless. No hope that there was any life left in the dying universe that had become my mental tomb.

This did not mean that my experience of my inner life or of outward conditions in hell was unreal to me. No, every waking moment was brutally tormenting. Sleep held dark fantasies that were even worse. By the end of my years in hell it had become my studied plan to work so hard by day that I was too exhausted to dream, then I would drink half a bottle of wine—just to make sure. I fully believed that what I was experiencing was the true hell—the dissolution of a consciousness that had failed to achieve growth into enlightenment and positive *trans*-formation. The *de*-formation was now taking place. It could only end with further loss of powers (loss of health and mobility, mental capacity, etc.) and physical death in hell. The thought of physical death in hell terrified me all the days I spent in hell. I knew what was waiting for me in the grave—an unthinkable horror. This was the ultimate torment of hell and there was nothing I could do to avoid it, only avert it temporarily. My number one rule was guarding myself against physical death in hell.

For every single moment of those entire ten years, I believed in the reality of the hell that held me. I believed with the same kind of certainty that Christians believe Jesus is alive: I *knew* that I had been judged by my god, slain by my god and had awakened, not on planet earth as you know it, but in what was left of my dying consciousness. My conscious connection to genuine life had been severed: Real people, real things, real planets were somewhere else entirely in the universe that is also god. This god, who I still whole-heartedly believed was the true God, had declared my excommunication, "Depart from me forever!"—and then carried out the sentence. I fully believed that I was experiencing the true hell which Christianity, through its mythological images, had been trying to warn us about. Hell was exile from god. It was a collapsing consciousness, entropic self-destruction. I was *in* it, rather I *was* it!

Fortunately for me hell was not—as Jean-Paul Sartre imagined in his play *No Exit*—other people. Many of my fellow inmates at Cherry were indeed scary, but others provided comic relief or at least a welcomed distraction from the primary focus of my fear and loathing—me. I am now able to see this as the true God sending the clowns into the rodeo ring to rescue the hapless cowboy from being trampled to death by the bull that just hurled him to the ground. One side of me was now a raging bull. I would later say that I had enough fear and rage inside of me to power up all the lights in Detroit! This was entirely unlike the person I had once been: the gentle kid who tried to break up fights and *never* engaged in them; the pacifist who protested the war, but never the troops; the quiet guy who rarely yelled or cursed—and quit golf "cold turkey" once temper got the best of him.

Now, however, self-hatred was a furnace of fury on the inside, always red hot, always hurling curses against me. I could easily have done all manner of violence to myself and fantasized it often. The only thing that stopped me was the stark, raving horror of what awaited me on the other side of physical death in hell, a scene that I had glimpsed during my suicide attempt. Later, I came to realize, much to my surprise, that that most hideous moment was when the devil's game plan failed. The enemy is a bully who delights in parading his powers and loves to gloat over and terrorize his victims. He and his team couldn't help but show off the torment to come. I am sure that the only wise God let them go too far, so that in His wisdom an implacable resistance would be anchored in me to the thoughts of suicide and self-violence that continually assailed me in hell. Our merciful Savior used this unholy terror to keep me alive and reasonably healthy, at that, while He put the real rescue together. How I thank Him for that! "Amazing grace... that taught my heart to fear and then my fears relieved."

Send in the Clowns

Relief also came in the form of being released from the "snake pit" and sent to a different ward at Cherry, which gathered into one residence hall the people from my particular county. Here there was no hope among us of a cure; but everyone cherished the hope of being released. This brightened the atmosphere by a few degrees. So did cigarettes. Cigarettes were coin of the realm and could be traded for all kinds of favors. Matches were another story; only the guards had them. I learned to play the game of deference: There was something sinister about the Keepers of the Keys and Matches, a threatening edge to their overtures of kindness. They wanted to be liked by us, or at least envied for their freedom and power but they couldn't be trusted not to abuse it. I kept my distance, refusing to cozy up, and only drawing close for a light, and always with lowered eyes.

It was a different story with the others. Less a few exceptions I grew to really like most of the unfortunate souls who were locked up with me on the ward. At first, as I mentioned, they were simply distractions. Blaise Pascal in a trenchant social commentary upon the inward misery of those who don't know the Lord or His peace, wrote brilliantly about the virtue of distraction (*Pensée* 136). Why do we love to gamble, yet are bored with the winnings? Why do men love the hunt, more than the catch? Distraction! Intense goal-oriented activity keeps us from noticing how inwardly miserable we really are. Pascal goes so far as to posit that this is why all people envy their kings, since they have the wherewithal to purchase endless distractions, thus indefinitely postponing coming to grips with their own misery. I certainly was no longer living like a king, but I was "enjoying" royal distractions. The Lord truly "sent in the clowns" to distract the raging bull in me! Life on the ward didn't lift me out of my misery, but it did make it less unbearable by providing personalities and antics impossible to ignore.

Reflexively, I just wanted to be left alone to brood in my misery. Thankfully, this was not to last. Almost immediately I was "adopted" by one of the craziest people there, a deranged man in his forties who swore constantly. This by itself was distraction enough, for never in my life had I hung out with such a foul-mouthed person. Part of me was fascinated. He seemed fighting mad at just about everybody except me—for which I was grateful. I never discovered the wellspring of his anger. He was so crazy that the root of his condition was probably past finding out; at least I assumed that was why he had become such a long term veteran of life at Cherry. For a while we were a team: He taught me the ropes; I tried not to trigger his ire.

It was much easier going with the two severely mentally handicapped grown men on the ward. One could speak a few intelligible words; the other could only emit great bellowing sounds. We loved them to death! They were too mentally handicapped to have gone crazy or to realize that they were locked up with a bunch of people who had. They *loved* everyone! If you needed hugs, if you needed a moment of distraction, if you wanted to be reassured that at least you still had a mind to call your own, they were the go-to guys. They went almost everywhere with us including the cafeteria, where things could get a little messy. They even sat in on our group therapy session. We treated them like honored mascots; we would have beat anyone to a pulp who mistreated them, provided of course that it wasn't the guards.

It was just the opposite with the poor, blind farmer who had sunk into the misery of entrenched paranoia. This was definitely a distraction, though of a negative character. He was incessantly whining about something, driving the rest of us up the wall. We would have given anything to shut him up—and tried with countless cigarettes. He constantly begged for them, but could barely see well enough to get one lit, let alone safely to his mouth without suffering a burn. Then it would come out, "I'm in hell aren't I? I just knew it! You're all a bunch of demons tormenting me!" Cue in the tears and maudlin self-pity— hardest of all to bear, which I suppose was because we had so much of our own already.

The same sorry sequence often erupted in the dining hall: "I know what you're doing! You're feeding me a piece of s---!" One time he sent his food sailing, one of the few enjoyable moments—the spaghetti was particularly awful that night. For once he spoke for all of us! No matter how much I spoke with him, however, there was no dislodging the paranoid idea that he was in hell. I'm sure you can appreciate the irony; I couldn't at the time. Where did this joker get off, thinking he was in hell? Couldn't he at least see well enough to realize that we were people just like he was—not demons with pitch forks? He would even twitch as if one of us had jabbed him. It irked me to no end that he thought *he* was in hell, when actually he was only in *my* hell and a bit player at that. Ironically, he may have had better spiritual sight than any of us. I have no doubt now that demons were all around us. I was *filled* with them—as later events would prove! Sometimes, we even shared in their fiendish delight, taking turns at baiting him, playing into his delusion. Those few moments were my worst moral failings in hell. I have prayed for that poor farmer many a day since my own recovery began: I hope he got rescued from his hell, too.

Speaking of recovery, we had three ladies of the night, all junkies, in forced "recovery" with us. They were locked down at night—for our protection I'm sure—on the women's side. One of them had been jailed after nearly beating some deadbeat "John" to death. We became fast friends. The reason for my adoption by them was simple—they needed a fourth for Hearts and "Bid Whist." This was diamond quality distraction! Rosie and her two friends opened me to worlds I had never known. Their girl talk, uninhibited by my presence (they seemed to have no inhibitions!) taught me more about women than a dozen years of dating had accomplished.

I was fascinated by their strange and exotic life as hookers and junkies; their ready wit and love of laughter; their ability to brave the life they led and the physical dangers they often faced. Mostly, I felt honored that three African American women had chosen *me* to befriend. I cherished their willingness to trust me into their circle for it was evident from their faces and the tone of their voices that they were masking a lot of unresolved male-caused pain. God was giving me insight into the pain of others—what a miracle of grace it all now appears! The true God was showing me *life* and opening me to sympathy and understanding of people radically different from myself. At the time, however, it only served to fuel my self-hatred that I was making such discoveries in hell, where it could do me or anyone else no possible good.

All of this rich assembly of human brokenness and resilience of spirit came together once a week for group therapy hour. I have never encountered anything quite so surreal before or since for that matter. I am not trying to make fun—to this day I cherish what was offered to me in friendship. But it *was* funny. Imagine a circle of chairs. Let your eyes move about the circle and you will perhaps cringe as the angry, crazy fellow who befriended me ejects some choice profanities to no one in particular. Continuing on you will see a "good old boy" who tried drinking himself to death after his wife left him. Your wandering eyes will then come across my three card playing hooker friends looking very blasé. Next you will see a young man who was sequestered with us because he was "criminally insane" (!). Skipping past the poor, blind paranoid farmer your eyes will land on a spooky skinny fellow who was never coherent and never still, eventually you will note one or two other hippie druggies, and coming full circle, you will see me. Oh, did I leave out the two severely mentally handicapped grown men? By all means they needed this time of therapy too!

At the head of our circle sat our fearless leader, a *very* patient and caring older nurse. Years later I searched her out to thank her for genuinely caring for us. I had no doubt that she was a committed Christian. She was. I know now that the Good Book says love covers a multitude of sins and I don't doubt that it is true: She had the love; we had the sins. She kept us well-covered, but who *on the planet* could lead such a group? One person would begin "sharing" about something, only to be interrupted by comments going wildly askew in another direction, then another, so on and so forth. We were taught in algebra that a straight line is the shortest distance between two points. Apparently, Euclid's axiom also applies to communication. It proved quite impossible for any conversation to go in a straight line and find a point, any point, waiting for it at the other end. I stared in silent amazement. Someone really sent in the clowns. I was clowning for the others, I'm sure.

Yet it angered me, deeply angered me that we were treated with such a patently futile exercise. Sure, we had nothing better to do, so as a distraction it was priceless; but as therapy it was a total bust. Had they called it a fellowship huddle, rather than a "group therapy" session, I would have been fine. It was the pretense that bothered me, which was incredibly ironic seeing as how everything about me was a lie. I also found it galling that geriatric "therapy" was similarly overblown. In this therapy, our assignment was to unstring the beads—in another room—that the elderly had just finished making into necklaces during the previous session. That way the cycle could repeat itself. It was so juvenile! Could the custodians of care come up with nothing better? I am sure this was a flashpoint for my anger at the meaninglessness of *my* life. But at least I was beginning to care about something! I was beginning to care about the people around me, people that to my deceived mind were supposedly as dead as me. I should have seen that emergence of care as a nascent crack in the armor-plating of hell. Yet, I was blinded by the demonic deception, unable to note these signs of forward movement, totally convinced that my life was over.

Time at Cherry, on the other hand, dragged on and on. Nothing stops the clock like being locked up. Days were exceedingly long affairs on the ward. We were always waiting for something that might break the stultifying boredom, the stale, empty sameness of each day. Our surroundings only added to this sense of deadness: The sprawling campus of ugly, massive squared off buildings had been built in the cost-saving style of institutional brick; the insufferable July heat blasted the living daylights out of any vegetation on the grounds; not the slightest artistic touch relieved the monotony of the bare walls, floors and corridors of our "living" quarters. It is reported that Oscar Wilde on his deathbed in Paris said, "Either that wallpaper goes, or I do." He went. We didn't have that option.

Boredom—mind-numbing, spirit-crushing boredom—is the common experience of Those Without Keys, whether in the state pen or the loony bin. Time becomes an enemy, your enemy. It refuses to carry you. It slows to a dead crawl. It plays an endless waiting game, holding all the cards. In such settings ordinary time was bad enough; time in hell was a different creature all together. In ordinary life, time is a river that is flowing—sometimes more swiftly, sometimes more slowly—but always moving towards a goal. The goal is ever-shifting: waiting for school to let out, waiting for summer vacation, waiting for graduation, waiting for dinner hour, waiting for release from Cherry. All of this waiting is actually a goal orientation that moves you forward in the flow of time—it's going somewhere!—even if it sometimes makes you aware (as at Cherry) of its painfully slow progress.

In hell time makes no such progress; progress towards goals is an impossibility for the dead. Time is dead, just as you are. It cannot move towards a goal; neither can you. You will be just as dead in the next moment as you are in this one. Upon our dying, time in hell becomes eternal—eternally devoid of life and movement. I am sure that the experience of eternity in heaven is radically different for *all* is life and movement there. Every new moment shifts into fresh delight. How different from heaven hell is! In hell, all surface change is a sham because nothing can change the overriding fact of death. Just as the French epigram says, "the more things change, the more they stay the same," so it is that every shift in hell only produces fresh torments; nothing moves life forward. *There is no life left to move*—this is an inescapable FACT. Think for a moment how closely movement and life are interconnected: We see, for instance, a bird that has hit our window lying crumpled on the ground. We wonder is its neck broken? We see no signs of life and we fear; then, the slightest shiver runs through its wings— we know it's alive! In another moment it has flown away.

A Light Goes On

The time eventually came to take my leave of Cherry, to flee this semi-comfortable nest and spread my broken wings. I had no idea how easy it would turn out to be—I had been holding *that* key in my own hand all along. I was under the impression, somehow, that I was locked up for life, so I had settled in for what became a couple of months, which I fully expected to become the endless years. That is until the day came of my mother's second greatest gift to me, life itself being the first. We had always been close; now, she was my last bastion of support. I still leaned on her for sympathy, if not for encouragement; absolute hopelessness renders encouragement pointless. Sympathy, however, I could still use, and I leaned into her for it as fully as I could. Past a certain point though, mere sympathy only feeds self-pity, never removes it. A more strenuous love is needed for that and she moved in concert with it.

Through her tears, on this day in early fall my mother told me that despite her love and concern for me, she could no longer "carry" me. She *had* to release me—I was just too heavy a burden to bear. Oddly enough *in that moment* I perfectly understood and completely agreed with what she was saying. The weight of my life was truly unbearable; it certainly was for me, and therefore also to anyone else who tried to help me. I saw no point to anyone even trying to carry it with me. This weight was never going to be lifted. I *wanted* her released. Through my dry-eyed tears, I let her go. *Father, I never saw it until now, but did You use that point of acceptance and release by me to start opening all the doors? Was it a Spirit-led step towards grace? Even though I descended to the depths of the earth, truly You were there and You upheld me.*

I must admit that it felt like a loss—at first. I knew that my mother had done the right thing, the needful thing, even though it was a hurtful thing. I know this now because there is a *good* God in charge! The truly right thing to do in one's own life becomes a good thing in the lives of others, no matter how they may perceive it at the time. I had no desire to drag her down any further. I sensed that her decision had not come easily and I was sorry that even in her decision I had brought grief and trouble. Still, I was left feeling emptier and lonelier than ever. A few days later, I had what I refer to as "my Cherry Hospital experience," the moment when light began to dawn. It was a true turning point in hell, though I didn't appreciate how tremendous that moment would prove to be until my rescue from hell many years later.

I realized with the clarity of a profound revelation that *I* was all I had left—why hadn't I seen it sooner? This *aloneness* meant that from this point on whatever kind of existence I was going to have before the final horror arrived was entirely up to me; I was free to become a player, rather than a bench warmer! For the first time *ever* I took full responsibility for my life. I looked around, assessed the situation and realized that, although I wouldn't be any *less in hell* on the outside, I was certain to be less bored. Don't laugh. This was a major revelation!

I had not read Paschal at the time, but I was on to him, on to the value of distraction mentioned earlier. I was about to put my hand on the throttle of distraction and begin revving up the engines. By the time Jesus showed up I was racing down veritable highways of distraction. I can almost hear a puzzled Christian's objection: "But wait! Isn't distraction the enemy of the saving work of God? Doesn't it keep us from discovering, through our misery, our great need of God; therefore it prevents many from finding Him?" Absolutely. Under normal conditions distraction is at its depths the devil's game. However, NOTHING was normal about these ten years—everything was twisted, inverted. I was already *in hell*, eternally separated from the god who banished me. That god wanted me to finish the job he had started by getting me to kill myself—through self-focused rage over my endless misery. By a strange twist, distraction had passed into God's Hands as a divine means of getting me moving again in the right direction—even though I thought all movement was hopeless in terms of escape.

So, now I had two major goals in hell. They became in order of their appearance, Rule #1: to postpone physical death as long as possible (it was still the unthinkable horror); and Rule #2: to stave off massive boredom and loss of liberty by getting out of Cherry Hospital and then never *ever* doing anything that would land me back in a mental ward or in jail. I fully believed that I could accomplish both goals. I was the only player left in the game, the only being left alive in my universe. Who was there to stop me? Even god had pulled out. *I could take charge.* I had already come to the conclusion that I couldn't make the important things better—hell would still be hell for me—but I could easily make other things worse and that included being needlessly passive. So I determined to start moving in any positive direction I could find. Since, my newfound direction was to escape boredom, I dusted off my bat, got up off the bench and headed for the batter's box. But first I had to check in with the coaches. The dugout still had a lock on the door!

I can only wonder what our psychiatric staff was thinking when I *asked* for an appointment and went in for what would turn out to be my final interview. It wasn't like me to initiate anything. If you ever read Ken Kesey's *One Flew Over the Cuckoo's Nest*, I was a lot like the Indian who pretended to be deaf and dumb, not the zany character who was stirring things up. The ward wasn't entertaining because I was there; I was the one being entertained during those few moments when boredom released its death grip. My strategy was simple: Attract no attention. I was passive under their drugs; I was compliant under their orders. I was a model ward of the state: "a Lifer."

Yet now, I was telling them that I was doing better, so much better, in fact, that I was ready to get out. Healed even. *What about the doomed, Doomed bit? Oh that? It's over. Really, I feel fine.* Here was another major discovery. I could lie and convincingly at that! At least it seemed so to me, since no effort was made to challenge my confident self-assessment. I learned much later that they legally couldn't have held me against my will—only the first few days of observation had been mandated. Funny, but no one told me about that legal nicety while I was locked up. Perhaps it was a test: Maybe just asking to be let out of the loony bin was a sign of sanity in itself.

I had a new strategy that grew out of this experience, one that actually worked—never tell anyone the truth about what was locked up inside me. As soon as it could be arranged, my parents came for me and I flew the coop, never to return. Once home I took the entire pill collection that they sent with me—mind-blunting (as opposed to mind-blowing) drugs like Thorazine and Mellaril—and flushed it. I never felt one twinge as three months worth of chemical bombardment left my system. "My demons" had evidently been dug in too deeply to be dislodged so easily. Apparently, they had been laughing at the chemical arsenal.

Crawling Back to Normal

I have invested a good deal of ink and of your time in this fairly detailed reminiscence of my two or three months at Cherry Hospital. The reason is two-fold: 1) I needed to explain the main features of the delusion that was anchored into place there which would then reign over me for the next ten years, and 2) I could write about everyone there with complete preservation of their anonymity. After leaving Cherry, however, I began by imperceptible stages to be restored to life and that always means other *lives*. I don't want anyone stained in retrospect by association with me! So in loving deference to the ones now tracking with me, this will not be a memoir of those years—not a walking tour as at Cherry—but a motorcycle ride, pointing out salient moments of interest as we go speeding along. So, what are you waiting for? Get your motor running.

First, however, we must pause for refreshments at the old hacienda, seeing as how I went straight home from Cherry fully intending to just hang out. I have to say that my parents were remarkable during these years. They never reproached me; they never treated me like I knew I deserved. But they did show me "tough love" by their own native wisdom, not the advice of a support group (there were very few in existence *back then* for them to consult). For instance they would come up to Duke in my final season of drugging and buy me groceries, but wisely never put money in my hands. While at Cherry, they had the good sense to hold back and wait until I was declared ready to leave, but always stayed in touch with visits and letters. When I came home they let me lounge about a bit to discover what I would do on my own. No surprise there—I holed up, hid out (from all who once knew me) and pulled down the shades. With nothing better to do, I quickly got enmeshed in soap operas, detective shows and professional football. I now consider this to have been my all time cultural low point. My parents got onto me in short order and brought the hammer down—get a job or move out. I chose the job.

Even there my father sorted some things out behind the scenes. I was to be working at a local motel as front desk clerk and night auditor. I, former drug abuser and ward of the state, would be handling *other people's money*. Naturally, the innkeeper had concerns, but my father held a high position with DuPont, one of their best commercial customers. Assurances were given. Somehow that was enough. I liked the job, though I still hated me in the job. Hell remained hell, no matter what. One perk of the job was that I could play my music all night long while I did the bookkeeping.

Looking back, I can only conclude that God is a "sneaky" God—there's no other way to say it. Through this job He managed to get me working with numbers and despite all the wild, tumbling craziness in my mind, I slowly began to recover a limited ability to think rationally. Math will do that to you—it patterns logic. *How patiently You worked—without any prayers or gratitude from me! You are the Wonder of the world! But You know that don't You? All along I was the one in the dark.*

After a few months passed and I had become used to the rhythm of the place, Dolly Parton and Porter Wagoner showed up with a bus load of musicians. I was no great fan of country music, though I had been with my brother to the *old* Grand Ole Opry in Nashville, not the shiny, bright new one that replaced it. My interest wasn't audio, however, it was visual. Dolly was the most beautiful woman I had ever seen, hands down. I hated Porter on sight, though I don't know why. As night auditor I checked them all in; then, after pushing my eyeballs back into their sockets, I had the kitchen crew stand back the next morning while I prepared an omelet especially for her. "Can I pay?" "No, ma'am! It's on the house." I don't recall how Mr. Wagoner made out for breakfast that day, nor do I really care. But the strange thing is I've been kind of fond of country music ever since. Wouldn't you know, even in this little episode, the Great Reconciler was secretly at work, softening the hard judgments I had made towards "rednecks" and all things "country" during my anti-war drug culture daze. "Sneaky" God was leading me in the way of repentance.

An Unexpected Arrival

Little did I know that someone far more heart grabbing than Dolly was about to show up. My innkeeper, a crusty old battleaxe, veteran of many years and many motels, had received a promotion to manage a new "resort" motel down on the coast in Atlantic Beach, North Carolina. It was a big step up for her and she wanted me to come along to help out. Just say, "Would you like to go to the beach and get paid for it?" to the average twentysomething and what do you think they'll say? I can tell you that even if they know they will find hell there, they'll say, "It's got to be better than this!" For preparation I would have to go upstate for a weekend of training. Knowing that two girls from the coastal area were going also and would give me a lift, I sauntered outside my parent's house and struck the most debonair pose I could muster. That's how *she* happened to come into view. One of the two girls was a cute brunette with a great sense of humor. To this day she is the only one I remember. June and I were married for thirty-three years.

We had no way of knowing it at the time that marriage was in the cards—at least I didn't; but then again, I wasn't playing with a full deck anyway. June would always say that for her it was love at first sight—she *knew.* I would joke that for me it was love at first bite—when I tasted her spaghetti. Romantically-inclined ladies beware—she had no idea what lay under the wrappings of this particular package and I certainly wasn't about to let her cut the ribbon and see the real present hidden in the box. Rule #2: *Don't do anything that will land you back in a mental ward or in jail* included my "vow of silence" as a corollary: *Never tell anyone anything about how crazy you really are. They will try to fix you and you can't be fixed.* Since no one could help me, telling the truth would only land me back in Cherry. The Big Lie was my best friend—this was non-negotiable with me. So I did what I suspect comes naturally to many aspiring lovers around the world. I pushed everything I could find that was unpresentable about myself into a deep, dark closet and locked the door. Then I wallpapered over it. And then I shoved a wardrobe in front of it for good measure. The trouble was that, *with me,* not much was left to work with. After you take torment, torture and hell out of the conversation, what do you have left to talk about with your newfound friend?

By now the distraction level in hell was gaining heightened speed and altitude. This was good—thoughts of June streamed through my mind, elbowing for room against the entrenched mad cacophony, much like a bird's song in a warzone. Nevertheless, I was being ripped apart more than ever; that was not good. I discovered new levels of self-hatred, guilt and shame: *She doesn't know what you're really like; you're lying to her; this is insane—you know there's no love in you; it's evil to take advantage of her blindness like this; you're a dead soul; this is foul—you're contaminating her; the universe will seek revenge.* That last thought was a very real threat. Although the god who banished me was gone, he had left me in a totally responsive universe, since everything in my dying consciousness was somehow mystically connected to me. I now believe that the enemy does have a limited ability to see God's Hand. Satan's team was hurling everything at me that they could find to get June out of my life, but they didn't stand a chance. The Lord Himself had put out the welcome mat in June's heart—and I knew my name was on it.

I now had a third goal in hell that nothing could shake— Rule #3: *Never, ever do anything to lose June or drive her away.* Somehow I *knew* that I was being offered something I dared not defile: Never again in hell would I find someone who could love me so completely, who would actually *want* to be with me. She had everything a guy needs a girl to have; she even had the indispensable piece *I* needed her to have—she couldn't see the real me. She was one in a million. I was absolutely convinced that anyone else would eventually see me and take off running. God surely gave me that crucial sense of knowing not to blow it with her, for June was to become a major part of His rescue, but there was no way I could guess at His purpose or consciously cooperate with it. Beyond any doubt, my future life depended in a very real way upon not losing her. We often hear it said that God will always give you another chance. Even now as a committed Christian, I'm not convinced. Just because He can, doesn't mean He will. Scripture is full of people who didn't get an infinite series of chances. They were tested and "found wanting." Evidently, God saw that any future chances He might have given them would only yield the same result. Completely oblivious to these theological speculations, I saw my chance and took it!

As it was I had to pick up my pace: I was now running to keep up with June, as well as to get away from myself. In those early days, before her buried depression surfaced, June had such a zest for life and laughter. We did everything together, went everywhere together, had numerous adventures—all the while, hell raged within me. I could fill a book with stories about her—just not this one. Know that when I finally did lose her, long after the Rescue, life became an ocean of grief. It took a very great God to save me from the depths of sorrow engulfing me that second time around. But He did. *How worthy of praise You are!*

Meanwhile, June reigned unrivaled by other concerns. By the end of that first over-worked summer when my innkeeper wanted more, not less, of my time, a rare ultimatum was issued: "Steve, it's either the motel or me!" I didn't hesitate to say, "Then, it's you babe!" The answer to that one was easy. Figuring out how to make a living for us came with more difficulty, but only in terms of making money. It was natural for me to work with my hands, plus I seemed to have an innate love of woodworking.

While writing this passage, I realized that I am trying to describe life in hell and it keeps coming out sounding pretty rosy. God, "sneaky" God that He is, was sending gifts and giving grace, all *below my radar*. I assure you it was horrendous on the inside, though many outward things were indeed beginning to shift in positive directions. Even so, nothing deterred my blind determination to believe that everything always got worse in hell, no matter how good it might seem in the beginning. You can't expect a mind under powerful deception to be consistent, to see the signs of immanent grace, or to experience a single moment of clarity. *One such moment would shatter the entire deception*—that simply could not be allowed by the powers that controlled me. The truth is I was literally hell-bound to believe that I was in hell and nothing—not a single thing—could convince me otherwise.

Even the birth of our two children couldn't shake these infernal convictions. One day June said she couldn't wait any longer to have children and that we had to get married. Of course, I took the next obvious step and proposed, but felt squeamish due to the moral implications hounding me. How could a subhuman wretch like me marry someone, anyone—especially the only person I really cared about? It was insane! I had no doubt about wanting to spend all of my life with her, but it was impossible for me to find a *feeling* of love for anyone or anything inside of me. I was evil, devoid of life—that was all that was left. The god who justly hated me had removed every trace of human emotion from me. Could I ever overlook or forget that? I wasn't *allowed* to forget. The evidence was with me every day. Just one teensy weensy little taste of any of the fruit of God's Spirit—peace, love, joy, patience, kindness, goodness for starters—would have blown the whistle on the whole demonic operation.

As it was I had to chart my path by "reverse reckoning": The Christian seeks to be guided by the Peace of Christ; I used anxiety and fear as my compass points. The greater the fear, the higher the anxiety level, the more certain I was that I wanted to go in the opposite direction. I faced my fears, then turned and walked directly away from them, *every time*. All of my greatest fears revolved around breaking the three Big Rules that guided all my decisions: Rule #1: Don't die in hell; Rule #2: Don't get locked up again; Rule #3: Don't lose June. Simple? It needed to be. My mind was always squirming like a frog on a hot highway in summer.

Don't beat yourself up if you haven't seen the "sneaky" God at work in this. The Lord knows that it took me a long time after my conversion to catch on. But when I saw it, it really blew my mind. Crafty Father God was steering me towards keeping His commandments *while still in hell!* Since He couldn't lead me by faith and grace, He used the fear of God and "the law"— neither of which bring true spiritual freedom, but they come in very handy for restraint and guidance. What I've seen very recently is even better. Rule #4 came to me towards the end of my ten years in hell and it was none other than the Golden Rule! By then the company I founded had a five thousand square foot building and six or seven employees and I needed some simple rule *with proven traction* that would ensure I kept our customers coming back. The fact that it was Jesus who had said it mattered not at all to me; following it would be good for business! *You are so funny God! I hope somebody tells You.* Me, I was way too busy fighting against all the insanity to give it a moment's thought.

Children, Love and Coffee

The insanity came to a head with the birth of our children. In my humble opinion we have the greatest children in the world. They are young people of real integrity who love the Lord, love their mates, love their work—my heart sings whenever I think of them! Sadly, this was not the case for me in the beginning. I was filled with unspeakable misgivings. The Pentecostals have a saying about the rising resistance one faces in living for God: "new level, new devil." I found this to be true even in my reduced condition. Now that children were being conceived *in hell* the demonic messages ran wild like rabid dogs. I braced myself for whatever might come out (I had seen *Rosemary's Baby*)—yet was surprised both times by normal, healthy births. Something about this touched one of the pillars of hell and weakened it, not enough to make me think that escape was possible, but enough to make me take note. Something inexplicably good had happened. Twice. How was that possible? The unaccustomed thought floated all too briefly upon the surface of my mind before being sucked beneath the raging waves.

Our first born, Stefan, was a fighter—he had to be! I was supercharged with fear and guilt, which made me overbearing and protective. He pushed hard against me, seeking his freedom, bucking for independence. It was a good thing that he did, but it was difficult for either of us to grow beyond these early patterns of confrontation. When Alisha, our second child, was born, a thought dropped into my mind completely out of the blue: "This one will be easy." And indeed she was—the path had already been cleared for her by her older brother. The pillars of hell seemed to tremble faintly. This too puzzled me, albeit briefly. I noted it; then, the whirling madness swept these gentle reflections away.

Raising children requires money, stability and love. Love was an impossibility for me to *feel* even for our children, so I did whatever I imagined that an actual loving, living person would do—at least most of the time. Nobody said I was perfect, least of all me. I have confessed my sins more than a few times to June and the kids. Here's a sample from a few years back with Stef and Ali: *Kids, I failed you so badly. I did this. I didn't do that. Dad, would you stop? You weren't that bad. Yes, I was! You've just forgotten. You're both going to do some serious couch time one day. Enough, we're not listening!...* I still think some bad memories will surface for them like creatures from the Black Lagoon, but the funny thing is in retrospect, I'm left with the impression that when it comes to raising kids, actually *doing* love seems to work better than *feeling* love. I couldn't feel love; so I went after doing what I thought love would do with everything I could muster. Now, I'm very glad that I didn't wait around for the feelings to show up, which could have been a cold day in hell for all I knew.

Writing of love makes me remember coffee—with great fondness and affection. It was my one "unmitigated" pleasure in hell, as I later came to describe it. The only way I can explain this curious dispensation is that some things slipped through the demonic screen. The best things—June and our two children—came through with a heavy price tag. Bringing them into my "life" *dramatically* increased my levels of self-hatred, guilt, and fear because from the perspective of life in hell, it was an extremely evil thing for me to do—allowing "innocent" lives into such intimate relationships with me. Now, from the perspective of an informed Christian understanding, I believe that the demons were savaging me with increased frenzy because they could see that June, Stefan and Alisha were intended by *their* Enemy as part of my rescue.

As you might imagine, I read C. S. Lewis' *Screwtape Letters* with more than casual interest *after* my conversion and heartily recommend it to you for its uncanny insights about the infernal empire's strategies to keep us all in darkness at any level of experience or understanding. I read it first, however, while still *in* hell—doing that is something I wouldn't recommend to anyone. It really rattled my cage! With admirable balance Lewis *thought* his way into truth, even truths about demons; I was foolish enough to go *exploring*.

For some strange reason my captors had nothing in their game plan regarding coffee and it became a safe haven, my *only* one. One piping hot cup of a strong, rich blend (*I'll take it black please!*) between my hands, breathing deeply the intoxicating aroma, savoring the taste and I could almost forget where I was and who I was. The demons didn't seem to mind my coffee love affair. Perhaps they saw it as an addiction, another stroke for their side! I gave it up as a gift to Jesus when I met Him—a freewill offering intended to keep me forever in remembrance that He now meant more to me than my only unadulterated pleasure in hell. Lest I forget who now holds my heart. *My irresistible Savior, You are worth more than all the coffee in Columbia, all the tea in China.* I have often joked that Juan Valdez of Columbia coffee-picking fame will be the first person I want to meet in heaven. Thank heavens though, I didn't put tea under the same vow...

The Timberworks Years

Making money came a lot harder during my time in hell than enjoying coffee, but brought with it a measure of outward stability. From general construction work, I moved on to carpentry; from carpentry I moved on to furniture making. June was instrumental in this transition—she befriended a couple who were selling frontier style furniture in a store across from where she was working at a mall. The couple, along with a small crew of hippie carpenters made the furniture in a barn outside Raleigh, North Carolina; the barn was located in a little community called Lizard Lick. (I couldn't make up stuff like this!) It was tailor-made for me (there goes God again). I got hired and eventually was managing a workshop/store combination in an old train depot in Morehead City where our kids were born.

I started designing a whole line of "colonial primitive" furniture during the mid to late '70s; we caught the Bicentennial wave. As soon as we made something, we sold it—right off the showroom floor, often with the sawdust still on it. However, this proved too good to last. The bigger the business got, the less room there was for both the owner's ego and mine. A thought floated in from nowhere: "An opportunity will come, wait for it." Sure enough, the right time came to launch my own business. Again, as with June, as with Stefan and Alisha, I shrugged off this obviously good occurrence, with the bitter certainty that, even if "the universe" was slipping up, hell was still in full force.

I took advantage of the momentary slippage, however, bought an old Willys paneled Jeep and made up some business cards that proudly proclaimed, "The Lone Woodsman—Have Hammer Will Travel." Pictured on the card I designed was a gun belt loaded with nails and a hammer in the holster. I *hated* it that I was in hell—I saw that I could have a great life if only I were still alive! My thoughts would rage: *I could be having fun doing all this—but no, I had to be a god-forsaken idiot. I had to get damned to this hell forever. I'm doomed...* It was June's admiration for *all* my efforts that kept me striving for more successes. Unfortunately, this particular bubble got popped when my so-called friends began singing a raucous version of the "William Tell Overture," the *Lone Ranger's* theme song, whenever I pulled up at their site. They would practically fall on the ground laughing—that put the nail in the Lone Woodsman's coffin. I couldn't stand the teasing, even if it was good natured.

So decades before Madonna would hijack the term, I "reinvented myself." Timberworks was born.

Shortly after launching Timberworks in an old garage on Morehead City's main highway, I got some chemicals in my eyes and went partially blind. The doctors didn't believe my chemical-in-the-eyes theory: One was convinced I had a brain tumor, the other that I had MS. I had no idea what either diagnosis meant—especially the Multiple *what?*—but I was by no means too blind to see that they represented a clear violation of Rule #1: *Avoid physical death in hell at all costs.* Fear camped out with me on the sofa. Adding to the concern, we didn't have any health insurance. When my eyes returned to normal two weeks later ("Say doc, what happened to the Multiple what?" "Don't know, must have been something in your eyes."), I set sail in a new direction. Until this point my inner hippie mantra had been "small is beautiful." But with two children, no health insurance, no mortgage payment and above all no washer/dryer of our own, I suddenly realized "bigger is better." It was time for this washed-up '60s dropout to rejoin the middle class.

With a short-term loan from a friend we moved into a rather large warehouse and I started designing and making a line of Scandinavian style furniture. We worked hard, but never caught the wave. Even so, distraction accelerated to full throttle. In no time at all I was operating way beyond my level of competence, but as always it kept me from dwelling too much on how thoroughly miserable I was! Hellish torment never left, I just couldn't *afford* to devote all my focus to being tormented. Money was flying through our fingers, but never staying on hand. That was because a small retail business in a feast and famine tourist economy, is like a roller coaster ride at the fair— a thrill a minute. Some people *like* living on the edge. June would say, "Oh Steve, he *loves* the pressure of doing things at the last minute." She was wrong. I didn't enjoy it; I just never had the clarity of mind to actually schedule, plan things out, train my help, or balance the books—things normal people in business do who aren't devoting half their mental energy to screaming curses at themselves for being dead.

Enter the Christians

I was so tenaciously racing along on the treadmill that June thought God would have to break both my legs to get my attention. Her theology was a bit skewed—she was a new Christian. Her conversion happened in our furniture showroom, so it was a good thing business was slow in those days! She was reading a Christian comic book about the crucifixion when a conviction hit her with the full force of sudden revelation: *She* was a sinner. She, who had been victimized by rape, needed Christ to be the Victim for her own sins. Jesus died *for her*. She cried out in genuine repentance, falling to her knees, instinctively looking upwards. Above her in the air she beheld an open vision of Jesus on the cross—so real it seemed, she was there *with* Him. Through her tears she saw His nail-pierced hands and feet, the wound in His side, the crown of thorns, the eyes of LOVE. When she arose it was into a whole new life—a stunning rebirth through faith. She had found a greater love than husband, kids or cats. There is no other way to say it: She was head over heels in love with Jesus Christ!

She would tell me none of this, however, until three years later. It would be three years of intense intercessory prayer—she wanted me onboard, and it seemed the Lord had given her a "burden" that wouldn't quit. Looking around the typical church and seeing so many Christian women of older years without their husbands at their sides, she cried out to God: "I can't wait thirty years for You to save Steve. Do it now!" Later, after my rescue when I learned the inside story, I had a secret reason to be grateful for her sense of urgency. Hell really was *killing* me. During those Timberworks years I was living with so much demonic pressure and so much business pressure, that I was absolutely convinced I was on track for an early stroke or heart attack. Due to Rule #2 and its corollary (the vow of silence), I was holding so much inside that I was jam-packed and ready to implode. What made it even worse was that Rule #3 (don't lose June) had me on a collision course with Rule #1 (don't die in hell), and I saw no way to get off that train.

June got onboard with the Lord as a result of the way God worked with the entire family after her father Tony, aka "Big Dad," died of cancer. As the disease was taking Tony down, some Baptists in the neighborhood reached out to him and led him to saving faith. At the time none of Tony's fairly large extended family were Christians: not his wife, not his eight grown children, not any of the in-laws, none of the grandkids; no one. None of us even knew how to talk with Tony about his impending death and resisted his every effort to share the hope in Christ that he had found. After becoming a Christian myself, I later became friends with the director of the funeral home—until then I had avoided funerals and gravesites like the plague. He told me that Tony's burial service was the bleakest he had ever seen, "Not one of y'all had a scrap of hope for a next life." Indeed, he was absolutely right: All any of us could see was a dead body and a hole in the ground. For me the bell was tolling on Rule #1.

The story of Tony's conversion went into the grave with him—until three months after he died, when a granddaughter discovered the witnessing tape he left for one of us to find. On it he told through the tears how he found God and now just wanted to "go home to Jesus." Then he prayed what I later would call his "high priestly prayer" for every one of us to be saved. God beautifully and stunningly answered that prayer. Hundreds of people, maybe thousands by now, owe their conversions at least in part to this man's witness and prayer which only surfaced after he was buried. Talk about resurrection! The cassette spread through the family like wildfire. There were no immediate conversions, but it pointed everyone in the right direction, everyone except me of course. I had nowhere to go. I was already at the end of my journey, a dead end. This was my message to June at the beginning of her search: *If you want to try to find God, I won't stop you. But I will be standing back, way back.*

To my surprise almost all the "safe" pagans around me in my loving extended family began going on a search for God—and in no time at all were actually saying that they were finding Him in the Person of His Son, Jesus Christ. I wanted none of it, but I couldn't help but keep tabs. My side—the Pagans—seemed to be losing. First brother Jim went over, then mother Clara, then sisters Betty and Josie. June went over as a result of the Christian comic Jim gave her to read (I noted to myself: "Watch out for comics"). They were all catching something—I literally thought of it as group hysteria—and I wanted none of it. It was getting way too close for comfort. Someone might gain spiritual eyes to see that I was a dead and damned soul hiding my true condition from them. I didn't exactly know how Christians felt about that kind of thing but I was certain it couldn't be good. Besides being a violation of Rule #2 and landing me back in Cherry, it could easily spoil things between me and June, the dreaded breaking of Rule #3. I braced for the worst.

One summer afternoon in the midst of this, brother-in-law Robert stopped by Timberworks for a visit. Robert was not only an "out-law" like myself (we married in to the clan), he was a "wood butcher" like me and had also been a hippie back in the day. We were even the same age, well, give or take a year. You can imagine my relief when I heard him confess his own concerns: "Steve, have you noticed how our wives and all these other family members are becoming Christians?" Guardedly, I allowed that I had. He continued, "This is getting out of hand! It's up to you and me, bro. We've got to hold the line!" Naturally I agreed whole-heartedly; right then and there I knew I had an ally. The sun was shining on our dockside sitting area behind my shop. Overhead, seagulls sang as they soared. Life was good, considering that it stunk, I was doomed, the usual. Even so, I could hardly believe my good luck—I had *an ally in the family*, a buffer against encroaching religion!

It *was* too good to be true—the next time I saw Robert, he had become one of them. In the popular Sunday comic strip "Peanuts" clever little Lucy could always manage to convince gullible Charley Brown that *this* time she wouldn't snatch the football away at the last minute, when he ran forward to kick it. Always she snatched the football. Always he landed flat on his back. Now it was my turn. Casting rueful eyes up at the sky, I remembered that hell also had its predictable outcomes; only it wasn't nearly as much fun *being* a hapless guy like Charlie Brown, as it was reading about him. This confirmed one of the unbreakable rules of hell's operations—no matter how good something starts out, it *will* go downhill rapidly from there. *Never get your hopes up.* Me, I had no hope. The noose was being tightened, even I could see that.

That noose was actually God's saving net in disguise. Remember I told you that June was praying, praying, *praying* for me to join her in her walk with Christ? She would later joke, "Ladies, be careful what you pray for. When Steve came to faith it was like Jack-in-the-box jumping out!" As it was, never again would she feel a burden that would take her with such force. She said she *had* to pray. She couldn't stop praying. She got TV evangelists to pray for me. She got everyone at her church, a charismatic fellowship in the next town, to pray for me. Some of them would pray over their pictures, then bring them to me to frame for them, secretly praying for me and Timberworks while they were there. Others came in more boldly. One lady had so much joy on her countenance that she positively *glowed*; it was all I could do not to run. I didn't know it was the joy of the Lord. All I knew was that I didn't have it and that it was far too real to stand beside without risking the exposure of the darkness in me. June went as far as Kentucky to pray for me which was quite a feat for she had never before taken such a long trip on her own. While in a prayer group there with her brother's friends, all holding hands, something like an electrical current ran through the entire circle. Every last one of them felt the jolt and threw up their hands in surprise and wonder, entirely convinced *that* prayer would be heard!

Wisely, June never told me about all of this praying going on around me. I would have shut it down immediately, if I could have found a way. I would have been *mortified*, which is a strange choice of words since mortified means "embarrassed to death" and I was fully dead already as far as I could see. Apparently though, pride was still alive. In the Bible we are told that death is the last enemy to be defeated. Scripture doesn't tell us when pride takes the Final Hit. In my experience it will need to be hit quite *a lot* for it to give up the ghost. I have also learned from experience that humiliation is pride burning on the way down. I was in a humiliating freefall for all ten of those agonizingly long years. But falling so far below the high point of my early years, burned away enough pride for me to finally open up and let the true God come in. We are almost there—at the point of rescue. But first I have to tell you about Eddy.

Along Comes Eddy

Back during the golden years, the Grainger High years in Kinston, NC, I was involved in student politics. I had even run for student government president and came in second, which wasn't as good as it sounds on paper since there were only two of us in the race. It was my first real taste of humiliation, of pride burning—and it hurt. Evidently, I had carelessly abandoned my school rule of *not caring*. Something in me wanted that position and it hurt not to get it, even though the other candidate was easily far better-equipped for the job. This all became redemptive. I was left with more time and, somehow, these connections made me known to Eddy, a fellow student at a high school in Plymouth, two hours away. Eddy invited me over for a party and a blind date. That's how our friendship began! We stayed in touch through the college years, though we went to different schools. Then when my life tanked, I abandoned all of my old friends—not wanting to be seen by any of them in my state of disgrace. I cut Eddy out of the loop same as everyone else. End of story, or so I thought.

In the early summer of 1982 Eddy was back. All of that praying and crying out to God by June *et al* had summoned forth a prodigy. Eddy was a born-again, Holy Spirit baptized Episcopalian with a dead-on prophetic gift *and* a deliverance ministry. None of that would have meant anything to me at the time, and because my memory is like Swiss cheese, I can't recall if I was even told this; however, I probably wasn't. What Eddy told me, much later, was that he heard the Spirit of God telling him to look me up. The inner voice was insistent. *Lord, I don't know where he is. Eddy, call his parents.* That was a safe bet because in those days you could count on the parents of your friends to still be living in the same house with—*oh-my-God!*—the same land line phone number! You could also count on them, not a machine, to actually answer the phone. Eddy didn't need divine guidance for that part, but he did for getting through to me: I wasn't taking any "calls" from anyone that looked religious or anything that seemed spiritual.

I was very welcoming at first—it *had* been years. When he started talking about Jesus, though, I began looking around for somebody to get the hook and drag him offstage. Somehow the four of us—Eddy, his wife Barden, June and myself—ended up in a cottage at the beach having a reasonably good time until someone had the bright idea to turn our gathering into a prayer session. What could I do? I joined hands with the others, closed my eyes and began devoutly *wishing* for it all to end. I had *no one* to pray to. Then it happened—something spiritual began moving among us, even upon me. Everyone got excited at once: They were delighted-excited; I was scared-out-of-my-wits-excited. They were saying, *It's the Lord, The LORD!* I was thinking: *I haven't felt anything like this in ten years. This cannot be good.*

This cannot be happening. I was convinced it was my former god, the one who rejected me, that had returned. I didn't know that it wasn't, but I didn't stick around to find out. I just wanted out, and I got out. June came running after me. We climbed into the car, and I put the pedal through the floorboards.

Fortunately for me Eddy did not give up. As shaken as I was, I let him stay in touch—more to placate June than from any real desire of my own. There were more phone calls and more prayers. These were mentioned to me by way of report, not prayed in my presence. I wasn't allowing that. Eddy was praying for my marriage and our business; both improved. *Interesting,* I noted. Eddy sent me two books to read. I read them both: *Nine O'Clock in the Morning* which I didn't understand, and *Mere Christianity* which rocked my world.

C. S. Lewis first gave the lectures that became *Mere Christianity* as radio broadcasts to British troops during World War II. Though a justly renowned academic, his purpose was not to instruct trained students of Christianity, but to reach even the uneducated non-Christian or barely-Christian general public. He got through to me *in hell.* I was undone. This one little book, in layman's language, took down *all* of the intellectual objections to Christianity that I had formed at Duke. When I finished reading the magnificent final page, I said to nobody in particular, though God was listening I'm sure: *This all seems so true! I'm sure it is. Too bad I blew it. If only I had my life to live over, I would want to be a Christian.* Of course I said nothing about this to June or Eddy. Rule #2 was still firmly in place.

Something, however, was definitely slipping out of place. All of my ironclad prejudices against the Christian God had come crashing down. There was not a single argument left to oppose Him; the gates to hell had been breached. But there was the seemingly invincible *power* of the core deception: For me there could be no redemption, no second chance. Hell had taken a hit, but it was impregnable. My mind was mired in the delusion, boiling in it daily, hourly—an ever-seething cauldron of ranting, cursing, fetid thoughts and maniacal imaginings. This didn't allow me to connect the dots: Namely, that if the truth is that Christianity is True, which I no longer doubted, then there is still a God *in my universe*—a God that would be looking for me with life and mercy to spare *if* I could just bring myself to turn towards Him. Eddy said that he and Barden would be coming for another visit once summer passed, when a friend would let them stay in her rental cottage for free. *Something* in me began looking forward to his visit!

Photo Gallery

The "Duke and Darkness Years" showing a striking contrast between a sophomore class photo from the fall of 1968 and a passport photo from the summer of 1971 when I dropped out to go to Europe after a year of "pursuing God through drugs." These pictures tell it all, but I was too blind to see.

The "Hippie Years" just prior to starting a business and re-joining the middle class. From left to right: a "wedding photo" taken outside our Raleigh apartment, trying to be cool in Boston, with newborn son Stefan in Morehead City, and Alisha, whose arrival brought an end to our freewheeling ways. Even we could see by then that it was time to take working for a living more seriously.

The "Timberworks Years" just prior to my conversion. Note Stefan and Alisha trying out the company's "Rocking Chicken" and "Rocking Horse" created with them in mind.

Post conversion photos of me as missionary, deacon and priest.

PART TWO: THE RETURN

Was it madness and insanity?
Or a spiritual battle I had lost?
Was there any way to get free?
At last I would find out.

CHAPTER 5

THE NIGHT OF DELIVERANCE

By the time fall arrived June was bubbling over with anticipation—Eddy's second coming was as welcome to her as the Lord's. On his first night in town the Christian family clan gathered with Eddy and Barden at the beach cottage while I was left at home in care of the kids, wondering how I was ever to survive the coming ordeal. Then came a knock on our door. It was June's mother Clara stopping by to see how I was doing. She knew of course that the game was afoot and wanted to sound me out: "Why do you think Eddy is here?" My walls were up. I told her, "He's come to try to make a Christian out of me. But it won't happen. My spiritual life is fine. I don't need it!" I was lying through my teeth—lying for all I was worth.

I dreaded exposure of my spiritual bankruptcy more than anything—it could only end by losing June. I was relieved at least to see that Clara bought it. My powers of deception were holding fast; perhaps I could fake my way through Eddy's visit too. In fact, I found out later that Clara told everyone the next day, "Steve will never convert. He's too proud, too arrogant, too intellectual, too stubborn!" She almost had it right, but her mistake came from looking in the wrong direction. She was seeing me well enough, but the shock of that had caused her to lose sight of the Lord and what He could and would do. Yet, even in her seeing of me, what she couldn't see was that crushed and beaten part of me hiding beneath the hardened shell. I was putting *all* my available energy and craft into the cover-up, though I desperately wanted out—I just thought there was no way out!

Every non-believer that you know is involved in a cover-up as well—just as misguided as mine, just as misguided as Adam and Eve's when they reached for the fig leaves to hide their nakedness. How can people who don't know their God, know their own hearts? They may have covered up their heart so thoroughly that they are no longer aware of their own deepest needs and desires, but God puts eternity in *every* heart. Psalm 42:7 speaks of God going deep: searching our depths to call us forth from our hiding places. When "deep calls unto deep" never rule out who may answer the call.

The next day, September 29th, 1982, is a red-letter day on my calendar now, but it began as any other typical, taxing, tiring day at work. I came home absolutely beat, in no mood for Eddy to come over, but too weak and weary to resist. Not only that but I had a severe headache, stomach ache, nausea and a sinus attack well underway and gaining speed. Looking back, I'm sure the demons were pulling out all the stops—they knew their Enemy was orchestrating an attack on their position. All I knew was that if I could endure a bit of religious talk for an hour or so, I could honestly plead sickness and make a hasty retreat to bed—the perfect excuse! June prepared spaghetti that night, a natural choice, but was she remembering it had opened my eyes once before? Was she hoping it would herald the beginning of another romance, the Divine Romance? I doubt it, but I'll ask her when I see her in heaven. Probably it was just cheap and easy for her to do. Far more likely, it was the Lord tipping His Hand, weaving through June's natural choices His own pattern and meaning. *Jesus you are so good at what You do—I never saw that until just now.*

After dinner we moved into the living room for conversation—nothing cheap or easy for me about the time coming up. It was time to pay the piper for stringing Eddy along to placate June. I seem to recall Eddy beginning the same way as Clara had: "You know why I'm here?" I tried stonewalling again: "Sure, you're here to make a Christian of me, but I'm fine. Really." Undeterred, Eddy launched into one of the most enigmatic monologues I have ever heard in a witnessing session. He expounded on "the seed," and for about an hour carried, or dragged in my case, all of us along with the patriarchs—Abraham, Isaac and Jacob—through half the Old Testament. I was so confused and worn out by the end of that esoteric journey that I really had no resistance left. My defenses were down. My body, under the weight of so many ailments, was shutting down. All I wanted to do was lay down. I was putty in his hands for what came next.

Suddenly we were back in real time. I was instantly alert and interested. Eddy was asking me, "Have you noticed that all of the family members around you have become Christians, born-again Christians?" He stressed that last part. I admitted I had—an easy confession. Then came the stunner—the simple question that began unlocking all the doors: "Was I curious about Jesus Christ?" In a flash it came back to me that I had never answered the question about who Jesus is when I was in college, yet even then realizing that it was a very important question, one that needed to be answered. But I had ignored it, preferring to seek a God who wouldn't interfere with my sexual proclivities as Jesus was known to do. Eventually it ceased to tug at me. Suddenly, impossibly, I began sensing and feeling *curiosity* about the question. *How could this be happening? Curiosity is a human emotion. I NEVER feel any human emotions. Not in ten years have I ever felt anything remotely human!*

Shocked by what was happening in me, I looked around the circle at three sets of expectant eyes, especially June's. I knew she was hoping I would go for it—that I would become a Christian, whatever that meant. I hesitated a moment, afraid that if I failed to convert "properly" my cover would be blown and she would leave me, as someone hopelessly beyond redemption. But in that moment I realized that Rule #3 no longer mattered to me—another marvel! Years of flame-forged determination never to do anything that might cause me to lose June, now gave way in an instant. Without any loss of desire for her, a new desire awakened, one that was far greater. I heard myself thinking, *If I lose her over this, I'll just have to go to another town and start over, but I've got to find out about Jesus!*

I looked straight at Eddy and said, "Eddy, I don't know what's going on, but I *am* curious about Jesus!" Eddy said, "Then just lift your hands to heaven and ask Jesus to come into your heart, into your life, and live His life in you." I did exactly that word for word—and heaven opened! Suddenly, past all wonder or explaining, I sensed the eye of my heart, something I didn't even know I possessed, opening, and with it I saw in a dim and hazy way Jesus seated on a throne in heaven. He was leaning towards me, reaching through time and space, and touching me with an effortless grace. Chains of demonic bondage and delusion fell away. Whole weights were being lifted. Hope, blessed hope, was rising in my heart!

Like lightning striking, my unshackled mind reverberated with received revelation and my own responses: "Jesus is Lord!" *Of course He is—how could I not have known it? He worked through all the years of hell to bring me to this moment of asking Him in!;* "God the Father is love!" *And I thought that God had hated and rejected me! How wrong I was! That must have been Satan!;* "The scriptures are true!" *Yes, and if I had only believed them I could have been spared all those years of torment!* I knew without a shred of doubt that I was being called to fulltime ministry in His service—though I don't recall His exact words. I also heard a voice saying that Jesus would be coming back in my lifetime. To this day I am not sure whether this fifth and final revelation was God infusing His thoughts into me or me voicing in my own mind a logical "conclusion" based upon everything that was happening. The first four revelations have all proven to be true; I am waiting the outcome of the fifth with heightened expectancy. Time will surely tell!

The time all of this took, however, was only a few seconds. In truth, it happened so fast that what was going on hadn't entirely registered within me. I remember lowering my hands after coming down from the heavenly vision and saying to Eddy, "Eddy, I only did that for you and for June." I didn't even mention the vision at that time! Eddy said, "That's OK, don't worry." He pressed on, "Steve, I think that you may need deliverance from some demons." I have to pause here because you need to know that during all of those ten years in hell, I would have argued until I was blue in the face that demons and devils were just a Christian superstition—never realizing that it was only by their power and presence in me that I had become so adamant about their non-existence! But my enemy had been unmasked with the revelation I had just received, and without missing a beat I said, "Eddy, I probably do! What do we do next?" He said, "Will you give me spiritual authority over your life?" Of course I said yes. Then began the deliverance.

First Eddy bound unbelief and commanded it to come out in the Name of Jesus. Then doubt. Then arrogance. Then intellectual pride. With each command I sensed something leave me. I felt myself get lighter and brighter on the inside—I was no longer being crowded into the corner! June later reported that when each spirit was cast out, she could see my countenance change—brightening, lifting and beaming. I became so excited I offered up two other "personality traits" that I now suspected of being demonic invaders: fear and lust. When Eddy cast out the spirit of fear, all the tormenting terror of dying I had lived with for years was lifted out and cast away forever. I received such an assurance of heaven that the hope of it has been unshakeable ever since. When Eddy cast out lust something horribly foul was washed away by a cleansing flow, leaving me feeling that my lost innocence was fully restored. Ever since then I have done my best to keep the door barred against both those foul spirits returning by studying the Word and by applying my heart to obedience. Good riddance!

However, one of the nasties got back in. Unfortunately during this moment, I began to question what was happening. I was troubled by some small feelings of doubt, and I voiced them, but that only made my insecurity increase so I said, "Eddy, I don't know what's going on, but I'm starting to have doubts." Eddy objected; he had already cast that one out. Just then Barden piped up, having been sitting on the sofa watching in amazement: "Eddy, I saw it come out, but you didn't command it to go in the Name of Jesus so it just hid under the coffee table and when Steve spoke words of doubt it hopped back inside through his mouth." Apparently they were coming and going through my mouth! This was my introduction to basic Christianity. I was a brand new baby-Christian being spanked on the bottom and hearing the celestial doctor saying, "Welcome to earth pal." If hell had been weird, this was wild!

Eddy then admitted that the Holy Spirit had been telling him that one of the controlling spirits—the main two were doubt and unbelief—had gotten back in, but he had disregarded the message thinking it was the enemy trying to throw him off. Thrilled beyond belief, Barden announced that she had been asking for the Lord to open her eyes to see this invisible realm, and now He had. We all wanted to know what the demons looked like. She told us they were the size and shape of little Smerfs. Later that night June and I cleared all of the Smerf figurines out of our kids' rooms. We weren't going to take a chance that the resemblance was only coincidental—not with our kids!

With that being settled, Eddy cast out the last demon that was on his "hit list" that night—negative expectancy. I was no stranger to that one, since for ten years I had been ruled by the very discouraging belief that no matter how good something began, it always went badly in the end. In all seven demons were cast out of me—*me*, the guy who adamantly didn't believe in them. Please note that they were cast out of me *after* I became a Christian, not before—and more would be driven out later. There is a mistaken belief in the Body of Christ that a Christian can't have a demon within them. I am living proof that they can. In fact, as a minister of deliverance I have never knowingly cast a spirit out of a non-Christian, but I have seen plenty come out of Christians. Christians are often the only ones open to prayers for deliverance, though they certainly aren't the only ones who need it. For their part demons don't seem to care about our theological niceties—they hate everyone and will gladly infest anyone who opens doors that give them right of entry. The beautiful side to all of this ugliness is how quickly they can usually be made to leave when ordered to go *in the Name of Jesus*. Receiving Jesus as my Savior ended the iron grip of the delusion; Eddy's simple commands forced the demons out as easily as knocking down dominoes.

By this time we were all getting very elated. I couldn't believe my good fortune—I had been rescued! *I had escaped from hell!* The impossible had happened! I was alive again, back on planet earth again. But wait, I had never been dead, never been exiled to an actual hell; it was all a cruel illusion. Oh My God! Jesus is real. HE IS ALIVE! Jesus saved me! I'm forgiven! I get to start over! People are alive! My kids are alive! June is alive! I'm alive! It went round and round. Finally, once I settled down, we all sat down, and I told them my story. Did that ever feel strange, wonderful, liberating to be able to talk about the madness *in past tense!* I didn't tell all the "gory" details of course. There wasn't time, and I hadn't the nerve. Only by degrees, as I saw I could be accepted despite the craziness of my past, did I draw the darkest pieces out into the light.

In the meantime I couldn't help but notice that every last bit of sickness in me earlier in the evening was gone, including a really bad case of athlete's foot I had for twenty years. So much of the Holy Spirit had come into me that there was now no room left for the enemy to operate. I instinctively knew that I was being shown a spiritual principle—that light drives out darkness; that nothing of the enemy can coexist with the manifested presence of the Lord. I also sensed that by an overflow of grace I was being raised above whatever "normal" would be for me in the days ahead and that some, if not all, of the illnesses would return. This would prove to be true, but I carried out of this experience the very certain conviction that there is a way to walk in greater flow of the Spirit, in divine health and in purity of heart. From that night, I have always been determined to pursue it.

Soon it was time for goodbyes. We were all tired, but it was a good tired. In parting Eddy said that the following day I should tell people what I had done and what had been done for me—that I needed to share the faith. Don't bottle it up. *Keep quiet?* I wanted to shout out loud! I wanted to hug all of my employees. I wanted everyone that had ever hurt me forgiven. I wanted the whole world saved. Surely if I could be saved, anyone could be saved. Had the Lord ever had a tougher nut to crack? Very likely He has, still He had cracked me open, wide open to anything else He might have in mind!

Jesus accomplished a two-fold rescue: He had just saved me from the hell I'd been in, which was a satanic deception; and by this, He was also saving me from the real hell that would have come later—the horror that tried to capture me the night of my suicide attempt. Amazingly, I was being offered something even greater than the Rescue: a life as His child, a life in His presence, a life that would now be leading all the way to heaven! From someplace deep within me I heard a voice singing, "Row, row, row your boat. Gently down the stream. Merrily, merrily, merrily, merrily. Life is but a dream." Somehow Jesus was reconnecting me with my lost childhood—I could *feel* it happening. That natural grace-filled life I had sought so desperately, while floundering as "Stevie Wonder" in the canals of

Holland, was being restored to me *as a gift*. Another wonder—the true Wonder had arrived!

Later in our darkened bedroom, June was sitting up in bed and I was across from her by the closet changing out of my work clothes, when Jesus came to me a second time. We often speak metaphorically of seeing Christ *in* others and there is a truth to that, but as I looked at June with spiritually refreshed and awakened love, her countenance morphed. Jesus Himself *was there*—unmistakably revealing His sacred Face to me and engraving it upon my love-struck heart. It took my breath away. I couldn't move while the heavenly vision remained in place—nor did I dare move lest I disturb it—and then, He was gone. I was stunned, transfixed, enraptured: My heart became His willing captive. He was showing me both Himself and the one through whom He had most truly come into my life. He was with her. He was in her. Just as He was now with me and in me. Without hesitation I gave myself entirely over to finding out where that life in Him *with her* would lead me.

CHAPTER 6

BACK ON PLANET EARTH

Meeting Mysterious Strangers

The next morning I awoke early, thrilled at the prospect of my new life. Just as it had been in childhood, once again life had become an adventure with every moment holding the possibility of fresh discoveries. Only this time around they would not be discoveries about "Steve as hero"—the supposed centerpiece of my own story as I had once childishly believed—but of Jesus, the true Hero and Center of everyone's story. I was a-wakening not just to the wonder of life, but to the never-ending, ever-unfolding wonder of *His* Life.

There was only one little problem—I didn't have the slightest idea *how* to live! For so long my every waking thought was "I'm a dead soul, I'm damned! I HATE myself! Idiot. Curse. Curse. What must I do next to survive in this hellish nightmare? Horrors—another crisis! Rule #___ is in danger! Quick! Do something!" It is easy to see that that kind of conditioning is not good training for healthy, happy living. But it was all I'd known. At breakfast I discovered that I didn't even know what I liked to eat—now that the real me had freedom to choose. It was as if I had been locked up in a foul, disgusting prison for ten years, never allowed to do anything, make any choices or understand anything but torment and bondage. All natural connection to the person I had once been was obliterated. Now suddenly those cell doors have swung open! I've been brought out into the light, a light that is practically blinding, and I am thrust into a sea of endless choices. *Who am I? What do I like doing? What do I want to do?* I was a stranger to myself.

This was a "happy" problem to have, but it was a problem nonetheless. How do other people deal with it I wondered. I could only attempt to imagine because I also had no idea what people were actually like, and I knew it. I didn't have a clue what they thought or felt or how they charted their own path through life. I had lived so long thinking I was dead and that no one else was truly alive that I had lost touch with any sense of shared humanity. I was now face-to-face with a sea of living, breathing human beings—people who had not gone crazy like me and who therefore were *entirely different* from me. They could no more understand my insanity from what it was like on the inside of me than I could fathom their sanity from my place on the outside of them. I could try to imitate their outward ways, but their interior life was a vast Unknown Territory. They were *normal human beings*—this made them incomprehensible to me.

To sum up, I had encountered Jesus and now knew that He was alive, but I also realized that I knew next to nothing about Him—the most important Person to get to know in the whole universe! He had revealed a lot about Himself in that first appearance, but He was still the Great Stranger. That was the First Mystery. Second, I had been restored to my right mind and had been given the gift of freedom, but I realized that I knew nothing about who I was or how to live my own life. Another mystery! Third, I had been returned to the world of people, but I realized that I didn't know anything about what was actually going on inside of them. *Yikes—I'm surrounded by billions of mysteries!* At the time I was far too frightened by this to appreciate what a gift it was; it launched me into a lifetime quest of searching out all three mysteries with freshness and passion. Not only that, but I was able to search with practically no preconceptions. I was a blank slate.

Fortunately in addition to freedom, I had also been given the gift of faith. The Spirit of God, which was now living in me, sustained me through these early disturbing discoveries with sufficient faith to believe that somehow it would work out. I thought, naively, that it would only be a matter of days before I caught on to how to live this new life as a Christian and that all of these mysteries would be solved in no time. In reality it took years for the fog to lift from only the most troubling aspects of each of the three mysteries; I experienced decades of searching before I grew into a more comfortable fit with my freedom. Of course no one this side of heaven would say they have plumbed the depth and that there is no mystery left to God, self or others. Even eternity will not be long enough for us to come to the end of that journey. Thank Goodness—we will never become bored for lack of fresh discoveries to make!

I was anything but bored trying to find my way through the maze of a now "normal" day of life. Have you noticed that life doesn't wait for you to catch on to it? As you might imagine, I was stumbling left and right, but at least I was running to catch up. Even so, being a "babe in the woods" as far as these mysteries were concerned proved to be a blessing. Ignorance is not bliss, but it does give you a tremendous advantage if you at least know that you are ignorant. Most people seem to ask the questions, "What do I want to do? How do I want to live? What do I think about this?" That just wasn't going to work for me for a whole host of reasons, the main one being I didn't know myself! And modeling myself after what other people do wasn't going to work either, for the exact same reason—I didn't know them. But above all, the biggest reason was that I simply didn't care what I or anyone else might think now that I had met HIM! So I started asking Him about practically everything,

"Jesus, what do You want me to do? How would You like me to live? What do You think about this?" This approach held endless potential, and it had the added advantage of being the only one actually recommended by the Lord.

For the answer to these and other pressing questions, I began a lifetime habit of going to God in prayer and through His Word. The voice I had heard saying, "The scriptures are true!" was none other than the Holy Spirit, our Inner Witness to truth. I wasn't about to disregard God's Word this second time around. Listening to and being deceived by the very convincing lies of the enemy made me now extremely devoted to getting all of my truth directly from God. I wanted to know all the truth, believe all the truth and live by all the truth that I possibly could—so *help me* God. Scripture says, "Taste and see that the Lord is good" (Psalm 34:8). Taste it? I devoured it! I cut my teeth on the King James version that June gave me for starters, then worked my way through and wore out a New American Standard and finally came to light upon the New King James. Now the pages are falling out of that one!

Learning to Listen

I have learned that the Bible is more like a treasure hunt than an instruction manual. Sure it contains plenty of instructions and we need all of them, but they aren't exactly laid out in the same way as our tidy little step-by-step manuals for learning the computer or making perfect omelets. You would think that the Lord would have done it that way. Makes sense to me, and it would sure speed things up. Unfortunately, He tried it once with Moses. Ten simple procedures for good living didn't even make it to the bottom of the mountain before being smashed to bits by the very one to whom He had given them. So if you want a nice, tidy, logical explanation for everything in heaven and earth, go to the theology section of your library for something written by one of us. But if you want to really *know*

God, if you want to fall deliriously in love with Him, if you want your life to become an adventure go to *His* Book. Just be prepared to do a lot of digging around.

One of the clues I dug into early on was tucked away in the little epistle of Paul to the Colossians, "For you have died, and your life is hidden with Christ in God" (Colossians 3:3). I sensed that the Lord was saying to me that I would never be able to figure out the mystery of who I am now that I am in Christ. That's two mysteries in one! The only way this was going to work was for me to stay "dead" to trying to live my life. In other words don't even try to figure out who you are now based on anything about who you once were—that whole enterprise was brought to death when you received Jesus. And be glad it was! Also, don't even think about trying to figure out who you are going to become—that is hidden from you by God Himself. The only way you will get to discover who you truly are (what you want to do, what you really think and feel, how you really desire to live) is *through Christ*. So if you want the real you to come forth, you will have to learn how to let Jesus live in you, and take your leadings from Him. *Isn't this what you prayed for My son?*

In simple terms, I become me—and you become you—by trusting and obeying Jesus. Period. Or rather, exclamation point! Only in this way can we become who He has created and redeemed us to be. Everything else is a self-made version lacking the Master's crucial imprint. But whenever we surrender the whole of our life entirely to Him, He can then lead us out of the narrow confines of Self into the new life, a life that is lived in union with Him. With this revelation a much needed principle descended from heaven with a KISS (Keep It Simple Sweetheart). As an old Baptist hymn goes, "There is no other way to be happy in Jesus, but to trust and obey."[2] There is also no other way to truly be yourself. C. S. Lewis put it this way in the

[2] John H. Sammis (1846-1919), lyrics: *Trust and Obey*.

final two sentences of *Mere Christianity*: "Look for yourself, and you will find in the long run only hatred, loneliness, despair, rage, ruin, and decay. But look for Christ and you will find Him, and with Him everything else thrown in."[3] These were my new marching orders.

A principle of simplicity, even one as good as this one, doesn't guarantee a simple life. I quickly discovered that it is by no means easy to trust or to obey the Lord. We can get it wrong on either side of the equation. The problem isn't in Him, of course; it's in us. In a word: *sin*. What a concept! That was a word that I never even thought to use during my whole time in hell. Sin got me into hell, or so the enemy had convinced me on my Night of Terror. Once there I never thought of it again. This is a rare "fringe benefit" to being damned and exiled to eternal death—you can't actually be *tempted* to sin. You have already *become* sin. It is who you are and all you are. You cannot *not* sin. It no longer is a thing to avoid, any more than a fish can avoid being wet. Surely all that was a thing of the past, wasn't it? Now that I knew and loved the Lord, I "had died" to all that, hadn't I? Much to my chagrin, I was about to become intimately acquainted with sin all over again.

Only a day or two into my new life, I was showering at the end of a working day, feeling just as dirty inside myself as outside. Knowledge of having sinned that day was heavy upon me. I have no recollection of what it was about, but since sin can encompass thought, word or deed, things known or unknown, things done or left undone, I have no doubt the sense of guilt was right on target. I remember thinking to myself: "This stinks. I'm doomed all over again. I've only been at this a short while and already I've messed up my fresh start. I'm a hopeless failure as a Christian." Just then the thought dropped into my mind like manna from heaven: *Do you see how the water is washing the dirt away? Confession, forgiveness and the Blood can always*

---

[3] MERE CHRISTIANITY by CS Lewis © copyright CS Lewis Pte Ltd 1942, 1943, 1944, 1952.

wash your sins away. And just like that they did! I felt washed clean and free all over again, and I realized that I was being offered an endless gift of fresh starts whenever I might need them. I later read, "If we confess our sins, he is faithful and just to forgive us our sins and to cleanse us from all unrighteousness" (1 John 1:9). How I have needed that revelation! I also noted that the shower is a good place to hear from God.

Hearing from God became as much a part of the treasure hunt as digging into His Word. Our God is not silent! Sure, He speaks profoundly through silence, but He also speaks through the beauty of creation, through natural events, through everything that moves, through people, through conscience, through inward thoughts and impressions. Listening is tricky, especially since there is plenty of static coming from the enemy, and the voice of the demons are almost always louder and more insistent. I complained to the Lord about this once: "Lord, I liked it so much better when Your voice was easier to hear; now it's barely a whisper." Waiting in the breathless stillness, I "heard" the barest hint of a message: *I'm speaking more softly now, so you will quiet yourself down to listen for Me better.* I knew to what he was referring and could see His wisdom. So much of my old emotional life was still churning inside like an engine racing out of control. Knowing that I was hooked on hearing His voice, He wanted me to have a good incentive for dialing down.

One of my favorite images from those days was of the Dalmatian dog, sitting in front of an old Victrola gramophone listening for "His master's voice." I wanted to be that well-trained. One day as I was preparing tea, feeling heavy hearted about something and wondering if I would ever again feel the lift of the Spirit, this thought occurred: *See how the tea bag floats to the surface? Nothing can keep the life of the Spirit down. It will always tend to rise—just relax!* I was so glad I was using a tea bag that floated that day. Again I took note—tea time and bath time are good times for hearing from God, so was bedtime. I soon learned that I needed a pen and paper next to my bedside because so many great ideas for what to do the next day at Timberworks were being "dropped in" once the lights went out.

What was going on? Why those times I wondered? One thing I noticed was that all those moments had something in common: I was not trying to think. Quite the opposite, in fact. I was relaxing, letting go of the day's cares, therefore, without even realizing it, opening to grace. Since we are saved by grace through faith, this made tremendous sense (Ephesians 2:8). An image occurred to me of a woodland pond, pelted by wind and rain, with all manner of leaves and sticks striking the troubled surface. How could anyone notice a little pebble being dropped in? Now picture that same pond on a totally calm day with a glasslike surface. The sound and sight of that pebble will be instantly noticed and every ripple it makes can be traced. Our task is to prepare a still, quiet place from which to hear the gentle voice: "I have calmed and quieted my soul, like a weaned child with its mother" (Psalm 131:2).

How do you do that, though, with hell raging against you, trying to get back in or drag you back down? Jesus said that the demons, when cast out of a person, will seek to return and bring some of their buddies along to add to the mayhem (Matthew 12:43-45). Already I had been learning how to nail the door shut against sexual lust and the fear of death, both trying to stage a comeback. Those attacks were obvious and unsettling, yet reasonably easy to withstand. The other five demons Eddy had cast out seemed so much harder to recognize and I had no idea how well I was standing up to them. I didn't even want to consider the possibility that there were still more that I knew nothing about, hidden within like "moles" in a spy novel.

Searching for Something More

Throughout the working day, I was memorizing scriptures like crazy in an attempt to "armor up," but it seemed like much more was needed. This was war! What had I gotten myself into? The enemy was all pervasive, highly deceptive and very determined. Why did they also have to be invisible? Why couldn't the Lord open my eyes like He had Barden's? That would even the odds. There wasn't much chance of that, though, so I wasn't counting on it. Meanwhile we were going to not one, but two churches: the local Episcopal Church in Morehead City that Eddy pointed me towards where there was a charismatic priest; and June's independent charismatic fellowship in Havelock, NC, the next town over.

That key word *charismatic* held the answer I was seeking: power. Holy Spirit power. Jesus told His own newly reborn disciples to stay and pray in Jerusalem after He ascended in order to receive power from on high (Acts 1:8). He called it being "baptized with Holy Spirit"; John had baptized *with water*, but this was something Jesus would do Himself by an "outpouring" of His Spirit. This baptism of power came to the early church on the great day of Pentecost, ten days after Jesus ascended to heaven. It came to the churches of our day first through the Pentecostal movement in the early 1900s and then with the Charismatic movement in the 1960s and '70s. All three times the Biblical and historical sign of it was speaking in tongues, power for witness and power for ministry. That last included the gift of "discerning of spirits" — one of the very things I desired most. I was particularly interested in getting my spiritual radar enhanced.

The truth is I wanted anything the Lord said I needed! That certainly included water baptism, for me and for our whole family. One month after my conversion, June, Stefan, Alisha and I all trooped out to the Neuse River with our Havelock fellowship on October 31st 1982. I loved the swipe at Satan that date represented — we were reclaiming Halloween (All Hallows' Eve) for Jesus. There is nothing like total immersion baptism on a bitterly cold day to give you an assurance that you've gone the full measure of obedience. We came out of the water feeling so cleansed! The kids looked like they were seeing an-gels. But because the pastor's wife—*on the dry shore*—shouted out that my head, the "offending part" as she called it, hadn't gone totally under, down I went a second time!

In the month following my river baptism I was hot on the trail of the Holy Spirit and reading all I could about His work and ministry. I kept hearing about the baptism of the Spirit and knew that I wanted that too. My Episcopal priest, King Cole, who was himself Spirit-baptized, prayed for me to receive it, but I was too bound up with fears and desperation to make any headway. I was afraid I might not qualify, or that God would withhold it, or that I wouldn't be able to do whatever my part was. Simply put, I wasn't trusting—that's usually our part. Sal-vation is a wide term, which covers all we might need to re-ceive from God; but I had already forgotten that salvation is by grace *through* faith. King said to me, "Steve you are so jammed up with this, when it does happen, tongues will probably come out of you like vomit." My heightened anxieties went through the roof. What an image!

Ascending the Heights

Sensing what I needed, Eddy took me to the true heights, a "mountaintop experience" both natural and spiritual. That No-vember Eddy, Barden, June and I were reunited at a charis-matic Christian conference at Montreat College on Black Moun-tain in the North Carolina Blue Ridge. It was to be three days of resounding praise and worship, incredibly anointed teaching, powerful prayer times and vibrant fellowship with hundreds of other believers, who were just as excited about the Lord as we were. *So, church isn't just for Sunday mornings. It can actually go on for days and you don't want it to end*—another marvel!

More marvelous still was what happened after the service ended the first night we were there. An invitation had gone out for those seeking baptism in the Spirit to come to a back room for ministry. Leading our group of twenty or so was an elderly Baptist deacon who positively seemed to shimmer and glow whenever he mentioned the name Holy Spirit. I didn't know much about tribal identities in the Body of Christ at that time but I was pretty sure that Baptists didn't believe in the gift of tongues or modern day "Pentecostal" experiences being available to all. Yet here was one who did. Not only that but he had such a kind and gentle way about him and such evident devotion that it totally disarmed my fears and anxieties. When he prayed for us my faith opened wide and I received a tantalizing sense of spiritual impartation.

Though nothing came out in that moment; fortunately, I didn't have to wait long. As soon as I returned to our "holy huddle" in the residential quarters, everyone there turned to me and started worshiping the Lord in tongues. The presence of God among us was so strong! Something about their freedom allowed me to open wider, and my new prayer language began coming out on its own. Almost immediately one of our new friends returned an interpretation: "Son, this day you have surrendered to me. Always remember." I have never forgotten that message or that moment in His presence. I sensed that the Father was not only affirming me, He was pointing me through this experience to a life lesson: The deep things of God only open for us through the pathway of entire surrender to His will. I was on top of the world!

Have you noticed that in the world of nature mountain tops and valleys always go together? It seems to be the same in the spiritual world as well. By lunch time the next day I was down in a valley, being hammered with my usual host of self-condemning thoughts and guilty feelings, which followed me around like a pack of flies. We were in the cafeteria hall at Ridgecrest, a Baptist conference center that was providing our accommodations. The "wilder" side to our meetings was happening over on the Montreat campus. Since Eddy was the only one at the table with me, I summoned up my courage and blurted out, "Eddy, I think I have a spirit of condemnation!" He said, "You probably do." I practically shouted back, "Eddy, get it out!" He calmly replied, "No, I'm not going to." You can imagine my consternation: "What do you mean? Eddyyyy!" Eddy simply said, "Steve, you can do it yourself." *I can? Well, OK let's see how this goes.* "Spirit of condemnation I command you in the Name of Jesus to leave me right now." Right then and there in the cafeteria at Ridgecrest I was delivered of a very pesky demon that had been inside me for years. *Oh, brave new world...*

I wasn't always so brave though. Riding down the mountain when the conference was over with Barden and June dozing off in the back seat I had opportunities to feel anxieties of a different kind. Eddy was playing a cassette tape of a teaching on "Brokenness" by Dr. Charles Stanley. I can still remember the teaching twenty-nine years later—that should give preachers everywhere reason to shout "Hallelujah!" from their steeple tops. The main theme was that God's Spirit often works best through the places of our brokenness, since anything that is hard and resisting in us becomes a hindrance to His more graceful ways. Typically we build up self-protective walls around the unhealed parts of our past and these walls become obstacles that God has to break down in order to use us more fully. He cited Paul's thorn, Gideon's broken jugs, and the woman with the alabaster jar. I'm telling you it made quite an impression on me—especially since Eddy kept reaching over to where I was in the passenger seat to tap me on the arm and say, "This is for you. This is what's coming!"

This worried me to no end; Eddy was my go-to guy for a word from the Lord. If I was under attack, confused or frightened, I would give him a call, he would listen, then pray in tongues and the interpretation that then came forth was right on the mark. Liberation always followed, *always!* Now, he was telling me about coming times that would be breaking me down, not building me up, at least not at first. Part of me was saying, "Lord, anything You say. I'm yours." Another part of me was looking for the exit. *Hadn't I been broken enough? Didn't those ten years in hell count for anything? Broken? I was pulverized! Come on, give me a break. No, I didn't mean it like that...*

It seems that we are the last ones to see our hardened places, but they are definitely there. We usually only see our wounds, sense our vulnerabilities and work at our coping strategies for keeping unresolved emotional issues under control. One day back home I was reading about Babylon and Nineveh, who were each in turn, the bully boys of the ancient Near East. As I reflected on their great walls which had to be torn down, I surrendered mine up to heaven: "Lord, wherever I have walls that are keeping You out, come charge my walls and break them down." It took a while for the battering ram to be prepared, but a few years later it came. I will never forget that pounding. It has a name that usually makes me pause, and remembering it does strange and wonderful things to my heart even to this day: *Honduras.*

Explorations and Exploits

This was still my season of "baby steps" and many pleasant discoveries abounded. I had taken to walking the neighborhood at night. I loved to gaze upon the stars and watch the play of moonlight on the broad expanse of Bogue Sound. I delighted in all the sights and sounds of our heavily wooded shoreline community. The presence of Jesus was so strongly with me on those walks that it seemed all the trees were bowing and bending, clapping their hands in the rustle of the breeze, as He walked by them at my side. It turns out that not everyone was applauding. A neighbor called June one night to share her fears, "June, lock your doors! There's a strange man prowling about." With a sigh that I can well imagine, June told her, "That strange man is my husband."

She meant it; I had become strange to her as well. June was both delighted and stunned by what had suddenly sprung to life out of her hippie carpenter husband. The old me she knew well enough—the plastered-over exterior I had been presenting to her and to the world. That Steve was a rolling disaster under such fierce self-control that he seemed placid and steady on the surface, even predictable. The new Steve was a cat out of the bag. My moods were swinging off the charts; my deep, dark, and secret *former* insanity was chilling to hear and hard to believe; I needed constant encouragement and regular deliverance. For instance that demon of condemnation I cast out at Ridgecrest, kept coming back to sit on me like a ton of bricks. It was hard for me to take authority over it and believe I wasn't supposed to feel so guilty, because after all I was always messing up and seemed very far from the mark. How little I actually understood and believed in the grace of justification in those days (look up Romans 3:24 and keep reading!). So I would put in a desperate call to her from work, "June, I feel so condemned." June, with a child in her arm and a pot on the stove, would sigh and say, "Oh, for goodness sakes, spirit of condemnation leave my husband alone in Jesus' Name." Bam. She'd hang up and I'd be free. But it was one more thing for her to do, and Steve being a Christian was supposed to have made her life easier.

There was a lot more work for me too. I was used to going at it ninety to nothing at Timberworks, arriving well before my employees, working through lunch and leaving only after everyone else was gone, sometimes long after. Now when I arrived home in the evening, totally beat and feeling like I had done my day, the Holy Spirit was teaching me: Stay in the car long enough to let it all go, and get the mindset firmly in place that my real work, my most important work, was about to begin once I walked through the front door. The kids would want me. June would need me. It wasn't about me, and it certainly wasn't about Timberworks (*my baby!*). I had a new assignment, my top priority: Be the best father and husband I could be with God's help. It was a very tall order.

Please, don't ask me how well I did. We men typically will hold up a better scorecard on our performance than our wives. Let's just say that we managed to keep our love alive, stay together as a family, have good times and grow spiritually—but not without *plenty* of struggles. That sums it up nicely from a male point of view. One of the great struggles was at Timberworks (*my baby!*). Winters were always difficult since our area's economy was driven by summer tourism. In addition to the yearly cycle that first fall and winter of my conversion June and I had been using Timberworks as a staging ground for witnessing to everyone who walked through the door. You might have come in asking only for directions, but you were going to find Jesus on the way out!

One day, a penniless young man came through that door; he was homeless, slept under cars and talked gibberish. All he had in the world was a half-eaten bag of Oreo cookies. It was apparent that he had "mental" problems as well—I had been in Cherry Hospital long enough to read the signs. We took him into my office and started presenting the gospel, then began looking for ways to minister deliverance. The Lord said, "Cast out pride." *You've got to be kidding me. How could this guy have any pride left? Look at him! OK. We'll do it.* When I commanded a spirit of pride to leave him, it was as if the roof came off the building.

June and I stared at each other in astonishment, then we stared at the source of our amazement. He was sitting there looking like a whole new person, in his right mind and engaging us in "normal" conversation. We took him into our home and to our church. Here was a modern, albeit tamer, version of the Gergesene demoniac (Matthew 8:28). Unfortunately, for our new friend, it didn't last. The spirits began stealing their way back into his mind and we didn't know nearly as much as we needed to about how to do a deeper cleansing or equip somebody to maintain their deliverance. He never fell back to where he had been, but he never fully recovered the freedom and clarity of mind he had first received. This was a crucial lesson about our own need for more depth.

The End of an Era

Incessantly witnessing and doing ministry out of your place of business isn't always the best thing for business. The bottom line was beginning to suffer; actually, we hit bottom and kept falling. We were at least $10,000 to $15,000 into the red, which was very big money for us in those days, still is. I was scared and more than a little put out by this. My complaint? *Lord, we gave you the business—and look how You're running it into the ground. We have even been tithing on the business as well as our personal income. We are in two churches every time they're open. What's going on?* My fear of failing was climbing the charts, but it was my fear of God's displeasure with my failure that frightened me most of all. Eventually I had enough, so I exclaimed to June, "I'm going home to tell the Lord exactly what I think of how He's managing the business. All you may find of me when you get there is a greasy, smoky spot on the floor where I was standing when I let Him have it!" I was serious. I had never stood up to anyone in my life. Now, here I was, taking it straight to the Top. Was God the ultimate Bully? I was too mad to consider the danger.

Once I arrived home, I entered the living room, threw myself down on the floor and cried out to God with full voice. I honestly don't remember what I said and it doesn't matter; it didn't matter even then. Almost as soon as the first volley of bottled up fear and anger exploded in the Father's direction, waves of magnificent peace began cascading over me, engulfing me, soothing me. No words, just a river of peace filled with love, understanding and acceptance. It was as if God was letting me know that He was glad that I had brought my complaint to Him and could trust Him with my heart.

Then I was gently shown in my mind's eye how so much of my activity those first several months had been driven by stress and self-effort, not led by His Spirit. I thought of all my frenetic Christian "works" and saw how riddled they were with anxiety to please God for fear of losing His grace and favor. He also spoke to me that His desire was to bless me and the business, but that *I would never be able to have more than He actually wanted to give.* So I just needed to relax and not let so much go slipping through my fingers in a vain attempt to grasp for more. I broke down and cried. I remember saying to God, "It was all chaff! Throw it in the fire and consume it. Don't let a trace of my anxious strivings remain in anyone's life that I touched. Only let whatever was of Your Spirit remain." I understood that many Christians may come to the end of their lives, see the truth about their mistaken ways and want practically everything they had done on earth to be consumed (1 Corinthians 3:15). Such is the stain of the flesh.

As much as it hurt to see how far afield my strivings had taken me, I was glad to be shown the right way to live. And to learn a new word, one that had never been in my vocabulary before: trust. I called in to work, asked everybody to keep going without me and camped out with the Lord for a week of tearful restoration, study and prayer. I saw that from the moment I had been spiritually reborn I had received a gift of an awesome faith in God—something I had never had before—which grew out of my Damascus Road experience of going from utter darkness into blazing light. However, more than Christian works, what I was meant to develop with it was the ability to trust God with all things, in all things and for all things—anything less was breaking faith with God. Without realizing it, that was precisely what I had been doing and it naturally threw me back into reliance on myself—on my abilities and resources, rather than His.

I came out of this season of deep repentance with a very converted heart. All I desired now was to live with His peace ruling over my spirit. I wanted Him in charge! That meant that everything else had to go into the fire. Long ago Isaiah wrote, "You keep him in perfect peace whose mind is stayed on you, because he trusts in you" (Isaiah 26:3). There it was—the missing piece to my missing peace: the trust factor. First thing "into the fire" was Timberworks (*my baby!*). I promised the Lord that when I went back to work my prayer was going to be "Let the business go bankrupt, but don't let me lose your peace." I meant it and, upon returning to my duties, I practiced it. The moment I started to lose peace, I would stop what I was doing, seek the Lord and often discover He wanted me to work on something entirely different. This radically changed my way of managing the business. By the end of three months the sword of bankruptcy was not only back in its scabbard, we were operating so far into the black that I was paying cash on the barrelhead instead of charging supplies all over town. Also, I was working only forty to fifty hours with weekends off, instead of seventy to eighty hours with no time off. Living by the peace of Christ was so much more efficient and effective than all my previous stress-filled efforts. Truly, He was managing the business *through* me.

Some Friendly Give and Take

It had once been my dream to have a Timberworks outlet store in malls all over the South, selling our handmade, original design furniture with its Scandinavian flair. This was slowly morphing into a Christian purpose. Since I had undoubtedly been called to some form of fulltime ministry, I began to speculate about how these two "careers" could mesh. It seemed eminently reasonable to me that the Lord would want to build up Timberworks to the point where it could support June and me for domestic or overseas evangelistic trips. Or perhaps our ministry would be supporting those already in the field. There were all kinds of possibilities.

One day the Lord drew me into a vision concerning Timberworks. I normally don't receive visions from the Lord in either 3D or living color; they are more like the original vision I had of Him in heaven—hazy, much like how the old black and white televisions with rabbit ears were hazy, but real nevertheless. In my mind's eye I was being shown a stage with two displays on view and another one hidden behind a curtain. *Let's Make a Deal* was a well-known game show from the '60s onward. Jesus was playing the role of the show's perennial host, Monty Hall. He was telling me I could have either of the main ideas I was toying with that I mentioned above—they were good ideas. Or I could trade them in for what was behind the curtain, a typical game show gamble. I asked, "Lord, what's behind the curtain?" *That's My idea for your future.* "Well, can't You just show it to me?" *The only way to find out is for you to choose it and then follow Me step-by-step.* Without the slightest hesitation I said, "Then that's the one I want!" How can life become an adventure, if you remain in charge? Additionally, I wanted Him to maximize His use of me. I never imagined that this meant Timberworks (*my baby!*) would go on the chopping block. But it did.

Sometimes when you give things to the Lord, He turns them around and gives them right back to you, just as Abraham discovered when he was asked to sacrifice Isaac. In the exchange we are set free from the fallen human tendency to seize hold of His gifts, seeking to be possessors rather than stewards, then watching Him closely as if the Lord was just itching to take them back. C. S. Lewis wrote in *Mere Christianity* that nothing that is not given to Him can ever be truly ours.[4] I have certainly found that to be the case at times. At other times He kept what I gave Him! My first discovery of this came very shortly after my conversion, when I vowed to give up coffee as a sign that my love for Him is even greater than what coffee had meant to me

---

[4] MERE CHRISTIANITY by CS Lewis © copyright CS Lewis Pte Ltd 1942, 1943, 1944, 1952.

during my years in hell. He has held me to that vow, though not by force. The tug upon my heart has been very, very gentle—He even gave me leave once or twice to go back to drinking coffee. Grace is good! But as it happens, *graced obedience* is even better.

A similar tug-of-war occurred over something else that I gave to Him with a vow. It happened several months after my conversion fairly late at night when everyone else was in bed, including June. I was lingering at the kitchen table where I usually did my Timberworks homework. Jesus came in through the back door. I have no other way to describe it. I didn't see Him with my eyes, but I could have pointed to His every movement in the room. He spoke into my mind that He was calling me to be as a John the Baptist to this generation to summon His people to repentance, and that I would have to live devoted to His commands and give up anything alcoholic. Of course I said yes. Who can stand in the manifest presence of the Beautiful One and withhold anything He might desire? I immediately gave up alcohol, but not without a struggle. In fact I took wine and beer back quite a few times, before finally deciding I wanted to find out what my life would be like if I kept that vow.

I am going to try not to leave room for two possible misunderstandings. The first would be that Jesus and God just don't want anyone to drink anything alcoholic period. I personally think that idea is absurd—it is not supported by scripture, let alone by the life of Christ Himself, who was actually accused of being a drunkard. You don't get charged with that for drinking grape juice! In addition, the recommendations in the Bible are all on the side of drinking wine; it's even used for a sacrament, just as ample vineyards are a sign of blessing. On the other hand, the prohibitions are all on the side of not getting drunk, except of course being drunk in the Spirit which is a different matter altogether. I don't have a tendency to alcoholism, so it won't do to theorize that God was "trying to keep me safe."

That would be a misunderstanding of why He called me to a life of abstinence. The truth is that He didn't say why; He only said that I was being called into a ministry like John's. It is well-known that John the Baptist didn't drink anything alcoholic, so I *assume* that has something to do with it, but I have learned it's foolish to speculate about things the Lord doesn't choose to reveal. Just obey. That proved hard enough, but once I settled into keeping the vow, the calling came to launch Healing Streams Ministry. With the Lord one thing leads to another, so long as we are letting Him do the leading.

The Good Humor Man

Being led by the Lord is one of my favorite parts of this new life, just as being misled by the enemy is one of my most hated. Ironically, you can hardly have one without the other. Following the Spirit is *always* a bit of a guess, because it is based on faith. Perhaps that's why so many want to confine being led by God to just following His written Word, as if that alone were all we have to go by. But the thing is that when you know exactly from His Word what you are meant to do, that is an *order* to obey, not a *leading* to follow. I don't want to draw too sharp a contrast between Word and Spirit where guidance is concerned, because whenever the Spirit reveals the Word clearly we are being led by the Spirit; and the Spirit we are seeking to be led by will never guide us in contradiction to the Word. However, just consider this: The Word commands you to give alms (charity) to the poor, but it doesn't say which poor person to assist or how much. For that you need discernment and a leading of the Spirit if you want to stay "in step" with the Lord.

This same approach to life runs throughout the whole of scripture. As great as His Word is—He even set it above His Name—God speaks to us in many more ways than scripture alone: We are guided by His Example (Jesus' life is a *visible* word—a word *shown* to us); His voice (a word *spoken* to us,

125

however we may receive it); His Spirit (a word *living* in us, however He may draw us). It is easy to see that there is a progression of increasing intimacy from following the Bible's words to imitating Jesus' example to listening for His voice to yielding the whole flow of our daily life to His Spirit. Jesus gave us—His Bride on earth—more than a book when He pledged Himself to us as our Husband. He gave *Himself* to us.

If Jesus had given us a "more complete" manual, I am sure that on page 3,157,068 or so I would have seen the *exact* warning I needed to avoid the bone-headed thing I did as a raw recruit. Only a few months old in the Lord and still wet behind the ears, I had joined a small enterprising group of fellow charismatic believers who were doing deliverance work with the hurting people in our area. June and I wanted to learn how to do what Eddy had done for both of us. Plus, we needed a spiritual "laundromat" for all of the people we were leading to the Lord, including our employees.

On this particular evening, our leader had just cast out the spirit of anti-Christ from one of my employees. The New Age was rampant in those days, and I wanted proof he was clean and in the clear. So I asked the Lord, "If You got it out of him, how about putting it on me so I'll know." Almost immediately my train of thought began streaking off in some pretty wild directions! It was no trouble to command the spirit to leave me, but I didn't relish the mind-bending thoughts ("Jesus isn't who you think he is...") and yucky feelings I had experienced (ego inflation, skepticism, anxiety, etc.), or the way the group was laughing when I told them what I had done. I promised the Lord I would stick to the way of faith in the future. Nevertheless, I was fearless, and I was learning. See what I mean? The mis-leadings, the learning and the true leadings all get wrapped up together in a package called "trial and error." As long as you take cautious steps when the ice is thin, you usually will do fairly well.

I wouldn't blame you if you wanted more guarantees, but only if you hold back from playing the game because you're not getting them. What *is* guaranteed is this: He loves us no matter what, has inexhaustible mercy for us, is the greatest Teacher in the world, and can bring a greater good out of whatever has gone wrong than you or the devil put into it by way of sin and error. It is also *guaranteed* you will make mistakes at this. So don't quit. I remember once in my very early weeks, going to the Lord in deep anguish of heart: "Jesus if You don't give me more of Your Spirit, I know I'll keep getting things wrong and sinning against You. I don't want to do that!" I'm quite sure I heard Him say, "If I gave you any more of My Spirit, you would be up here with Me and I want you down there!"

What can I say? Guidance is on-the-job training and the Lord is used to having to provide it for us. Here's an encouraging fact from history: The very year Babe Ruth set the longest lasting homerun record was the same year he led his league in strikeouts (1923). So keep swinging. The Father loves it! He played an image in my mind once when I was grousing about how bad my batting average seemed to be. *Had I ever jumped out of bed as a child on a fine Saturday morning and ran to my parents so they could assign me chores for the day?* They would have dropped dead if I had. I ate quickly and raced out the door before they could nab me. *So don't you think I'm very pleased when any of My children run to Me asking what I would like them to be doing each day?* I love His sense of perspective!

I also needed guidance when it came to speaking in groups. I was terribly shy and had been my whole life. But I "knew" that the Lord might give me something to share and—despite my fears—I truly wanted Him to use me in that way. So I would pray, pray, *pray* whenever these opportunities came around. In the beginning the guidance was tremendous—the word would come insistently, my heart would pound, my whole body would tense, the Holy Spirit would practically shake me until finally I would speak it out. People seemed to appreciate it. This was great! After a while though the usual signs and symptoms diminished. I would walk out without sharing, then feel deflated for missing the opportunity. So I carried my question to the Lord, "Why aren't You letting me know the word was from You like You used to? You know—the shake, shake thing." His reply? *Do you really want Me to shake you like that all your life?* He explained that He had been shaking me in the manner He had in order to get my attention *in the beginning,* but wouldn't it be better for me to learn how to live by more gentle prompts? I laughed in complete agreement.

Nobody makes me smile more or laugh more than Jesus. He can be so funny! One day I was driving through traffic and praying away in tongues. I was frankly bored with the few words I had in my prayer language, so I just started making up sounds and threw them into the mix hoping they would work. Immediately the words formed in my mind: *What did you just say?* "I don't know. I thought You would know." *No, it was just gibberish. I was hoping you could tell Me!* I broke up laughing over that one and had to fight to stay in my lane! He so often corrects me with humor and interrupts my thoughts with humor that I am amazed how believers can be so sheepish in saying things like, "Well, I *think* God has a sense of humor." Really? All we have to do is look in the mirror to get it. He made us *in His Image* and that surely includes loving a good laugh just as much as we do—or rather, infinitely more. Trust me, at least on this one: I have proof!

When I came to faith the only kind of humor I had going for me was sarcasm. I really did have absolutely nothing to laugh about during those years in hell, unless it was in a mean-spirited way, which I knew not to put on display very often. Obviously, sarcasm and cutting remarks are not the Lord's kind of humor. His playfulness makes everyone want to laugh and join in—no one is ever made to bear the brunt of His jokes. So I committed my sarcasm to the flames. I told Him I would nail my tongue to the cross where that was concerned, and from henceforth I would just have to be the un-funniest guy in the room, unless He did something about it.

One day in a Christian meeting, praying for "a word" as usual—something that I was always dead serious about—I saw some words go by my mind's eye as if on a ticker tape; they were so apropos to what was going on that I had to laugh inside. Then the thought occurred to me, *Why not share it with the group?* Which is exactly what I did, and everyone broke into gales of laughter. My new career in Christian comedy was born! Just kidding. My gift of humor isn't *that* good, but it is light years beyond what I had, and best of all, it flows with an effortless grace since it is coming from Him. That's how I *know* that God has a sense of humor. Because I do—now that He lives in me.

"Early Retirement" and a Move

I could never find any humor in my testimony, however. Every time I tried to share about those "lost" years, all of the hurt and anguish would come surging to the surface. I had lost so much! In my mind I had not been alive for the whole decade of my twenties, the birth of our kids, or my life with June. I had been robbed by an enemy who had hated me without cause (Lamentations 3:52). I hated myself as well—hated that I had "ruined" my life; hated that I had so much damage left to work through; hated that I still felt so weird and un-human. Although my new life of faith was genuine, this feeling of not "being human" was very troubling. It persisted even through seminary and well into my years as a parish priest. I didn't dare speak about it to anyone except June. She could always be counted on to love me, even when she couldn't understand me; still, my deep darkness troubled her, so I locked most of it away.

The testimony I shared was edited for public consumption, but it was very rawboned nevertheless; I tried to keep everything about my life in the past tense. Most Christians seemed to like hearing about what I had gone through—it was an encouragement to them. However, I quickly discovered that if you unwisely open your still raw and bleeding wounds you can get stuck in them and have a hard time finding a graceful way (translate that to "face-saving" way) back out. My experiences also proved useful as an aid for evangelizing the lost. Even though I didn't put all of my story out there, it certainly helped me emotionally to get as much as I could out in the open, and find the God-graced wonder of acceptance. I really loved being able to testify to the goodness of the Lord and the terrible reality of the dark powers. But I had no testimony of victory over the emotional wreckage hell left in its wake—and I knew it.

The more I shared my story, therefore, the more I felt alienated from any sense of common humanity. I became concerned that I might end up on some kind of church "testimony circuit." My story is unique, even bizarre with plenty of high drama; this began to make me sought after. I knew, however, that I didn't have anywhere near sufficient healing to walk under the pressure and scrutiny of a public ministry. I could barely live my daily life as it was! It would take me days of interior labor just to get my insides ready for one hour of public time. So, I began to shift the focus of my teaching style from me and what I had gone through in my past to Jesus and what the Word could teach us all about how to move forward into His future. This is what I now call the 80/20 principle of balanced teaching: 80 percent truths about God and 20 percent stories about you. People love to hear about our exploits, but when they experience trials themselves, it will be God's truth—not our testimonies—that will come to their rescue.

What I have seen of other ministers falling from grace, whose un-mended interior made them prey to the enemy, has since convinced me that I made the right decision to lead a more quiet life and allow time for growth. Working over the years with many men in addiction recovery I have learned that there is a tremendous difference between the testimony of an initial deliverance by Jesus and the testimony of an enduring victory. I knew I needed a much better track record of enduring victories before drawing *any focus* back on myself. We are stewards of our own testimonies. There is a time to pour the wine, which I did, and there is a time to let it mature in the cask. I chose to quietly retire my testimony. I hope I moved with the proper seasons.

Speaking of moving, June and I went back and forth about where to attend church. Going to two churches, with one being twenty miles away in another town, can make life with young children very hectic. It was difficult not to lose our religion before arriving at the church doors on Sunday morning! So we prayed and sought the Lord, and we thought we heard from Him. June's charismatic fellowship won hands down over the charismatic Episcopal church Eddy had pointed me towards. In retrospect that decision was heavily one-sided since the informal, free-form ways of her fellowship were totally in keeping with our hippie values and background. It was a very comfortable fit. However, I had told the Lord that I didn't care which denomination He might place us in—I was in it for service to Him, not self-service. He took me up on my word; He has a way of doing that.

No sooner than we had announced our decision to all our friends at both churches did the Lord reverse it. Peter Marshall Jr., son of the famous Scottish preacher and heir to his mother Catherine's writing abilities, came to the Episcopal Church on a preaching mission we attended. At one point he said he believed that the Lord was going to be gathering the scattered members of the charismatic movement back into the old Protestant mainlines. I understood what he meant too well—most of our friends at the charismatic assembly had been given the "left foot of fellowship" by their Protestant churches when they came into the baptism in the Spirit and didn't keep a lid on it. It's hard to keep quiet about something this good! Naturally you want everyone to know what is available to them. Turns out, however, not everyone wants to know.

As if to emphasize Peter's message the Lord gave me a vision. I saw that our charismatic fellowship was like a Leer jet — small, lightweight, maneuverable, able to rise fast and streak through the heights, but easily blown about by the winds of doctrine (Ephesians 4:14). The Episcopal Church, on the other hand, appeared as an old freight train with a good set of tracks that had weathered satanic attacks for centuries. It didn't have much of a head of steam, but if ever powered up, it would be able to haul a great load. I have probably offended people on both sides with that image, but it spoke to me at the time. We sensed that we needed the structure and stability that the Episcopal Church could and did provide. So, we became Episcopalians, but our heart for worship and for supernatural ministry forever remained charismatic.

The Lord gave one other vision to me through Peter Marshall's ministry that fall. I had been struggling in a way not at all uncommon for new Christians. I was trying to clean up my sinful interior once and for all. Peter counseled and prayed with me. That night I saw it plainly for the first time — the thoughts and wrong desires of the flesh were like "a river of filth" running through me. It could never be "cleaned up." The only thing to do was to avoid walking in it by yielding to the Lord and walking in His Spirit instead. I told Peter about my vision the next day. He was so taken with the image that he made it a part of his message, which both delighted and embarrassed me at the same time. I mean, how would you like all of your friends to know that there is a river of filth inside you? Of course they have one of their own to deal with. We all do. Why deny it? The Lord has "told all" in His Word. Even so, it is very liberating to realize that God sees our interior "sewer" too and far from holding it against us, He helps us avoid falling into it and cleanses us when we do. What He doesn't do is remove it, at least not in this life. He leaves it in us for our own good: It keeps us humble.

Zoom, Zoom

It's time to get back on our bikes for a motorcycle tour of the unfolding years. The purpose of this book is not to tell all the stories of my life in Christ. There have been many spiritual lessons and adventures, many fascinating people encountered, many sightings of our Illusive Quarry on this quest to know our God. Some of the funniest can be seen as short videos on our Youtube channel; others have been salted throughout our workbook, *Matters of the Heart*; still more wind up on Facebook as anecdotes or on our website as blog posts.

I have written as much as I have of the beginning of my journey for two reasons. First, for non-Christians it will have given you some idea of how truly radical and unsettling a genuine conversion to Christ can be—it turns everything upside down! Second, for Christians, especially those who are trying to fly with broken wings, I pray it will give you hope that if you keep pressing in to know the Lord, He will be able to lead you just as He has me. Not without mistakes of course. Never without pain and problems. But inevitably and purposefully. So an extended beginning was necessary to set the stage. What I really want to take you into is the amazing journey of healing that the Lord took me through. In a sense that has been the purpose of this whole book.

With that in mind, let's take a quick spin around the track so you can have a feel for the timeline. I came to faith on the evening of September 29, 1982 at the age of thirty-three. Within a month I was baptized in water; within two months I was baptized in the Spirit. After a year we had become Episcopalians; after two years I was completing my undergraduate degree in preparation for seminary, and after three years I was "in the process" as a postulant for ordination to the priesthood. That process hit a roadblock when I was told to wait a year before continuing—they apparently thought I needed more time to test the calling. So, during that time, June and I looked to the mission field to make the most of the delay. By the spring of 1985 we had sold our business, sold our home, sold our vehicles and were heading off with our kids (we didn't sell them) to missionary training with the South American Missionary Society of the Episcopal Church (SAMS-USA). Our assignment? Honduras. When we were asked if we wanted to go there to work with an orphanage, we exclaimed, "Perfect!," then raced off to get our hands on a map so we could find out where in the world Honduras was!

For an unforgettable, life-changing year, we lived and worked in the Honduran capital, Tegucigalpa, from late August 1985 to early June 1986. It was not all sweetness and light, however. Shortly after arrival June sank into culture shock and deep depression, one that hounded her for decades. Then near the end of our term, I almost died of typhoid fever which crippled my health for years afterwards. We were both broken wide open by these experiences. Although they ultimately carried us into places inside ourselves and upwards into God that we might never have known without them, the initial effect greatly reduced our capacity to enjoy life and pursue the Lord. I believe this was the season of "breaking" that Eddy and Dr. Stanley tried to prepare me for during that unsettling descent from Montreat. Honduras in Spanish means "the depths": It certainly became that for us.

Even though I had led all but one of my students to the Lord, I still came back feeling like a failure, especially for not having been able to spare June her suffering. This took me into my unhealed depths. I pulled back from many of my previous pursuits and sought the Lord for a deeper healing than Bible studies and deliverance sessions had so far been able to produce in me. I was dead certain that June and I were not alone in being dragged down into spiritual ineffectiveness due to our pre-Christian wounds. I began to be gently haunted by Jeremiah's warning to shepherds who "healed the wound of my people lightly, saying, 'Peace, peace,' when there is no peace" (Jeremiah 6:14). I wanted to make sure that I had strong medicine in the Lord with which to help others, and that meant I was going to have to find it and take it myself. I told a friend who was concerned about my withdrawal that I was convinced that the Lord "didn't intend to serve this wine until it's time." It seemed clever; I hoped it was also true.

In the fall of 1986 I moved us to Greenville, NC, and enrolled at East Carolina University for training as a high school teacher. The door was still closed to seminary, closed even more firmly now that both June and my Episcopal priest were saying "*No-Never!*" to the idea. I thought that being trained as a teacher would help train me in things I would need as a priest. It was also something positive to be doing while I waited for that journey to begin. Apparently I thought wrong. While fasting and praying one week, the Lord spoke to me almost out loud, *What are you doing here?* "The doors are all closed back home." *I told you to stay there and wait. I will open them.* We returned to the coast and waited. Three years later, without any effort on my part, all the doors swung open and away we went.

Seminary like Honduras could almost be a book in itself—it certainly still speaks volumes to me. However, in keeping with this "motorcycle tour" outline of the journey, let's just say that upon arrival at seminary all but one of the professors voted *against* the idea of ordaining me; but by graduation, all but one professor voted *in favor* of ordaining me. I tried to learn all that I could from the classrooms, but in retrospect, it was the "school of the Holy Spirit" which played the key role in my formation as a priest. The Lord has His own program for instruction and it is often widely at variance with our ideas about how things should go. "Sneaky" God, remember? Upon graduation we landed on our feet with an offer for me to work as an Assistant Rector at the "Mother Church" of Georgia, Christ

Church in Savannah. Usually a new priest only stays in his or her first parish for a year or two, at the most, before moving on to an assignment that "fits" better. We stayed for thirteen and a half years! It was a very good fit right from the beginning.

Too comfortable a fit, however, can be the enemy of the spiritual life. The Lord, who is Himself the God of All Comfort, seems to take a pretty dim view of His people resting "on the lees" and turning aside from the ever-challenging task of pressing in to know Him and serve Him at levels *beyond* their comfort zones. I always knew that the Lord had not shaped me and formed me for parish service, but had placed me in it to "learn the ropes," while He was readying me for some kind of "out of the box" ministry. I began earnestly seeking Him for direction and timing. One day in the late spring of 2005 I distinctly heard Him say, "I'm calling you out." I looked Him in the eye so to speak and said, "You don't have to say that twice!" That afternoon I broke the news to June who was surprisingly all onboard with the idea of launching a healing ministry. We fasted and prayed, sought the wisdom of our closest friends, received further vision, quit a perfectly good *paying* job and stepped way out there in faith. Healing Streams was born.

CHAPTER 7

JOURNEY TO HEALING

Getting to the Heart of Things

Until now I have been showing you elements of growth in what I call "basic discipleship": searching the scriptures for truth, listening for His voice, trusting *and* obeying your new Life Manager, throwing things into the fire, seeking to liberate others and pursuing your destined future by pursuing Him. These are tremendous things to be doing! There are more elements in addition to those I mentioned, and I am immensely excited about every aspect of basic discipleship—they are a lifeline to God! If you have been badly damaged and have a wounded heart, you need to be practicing all of these things— as if your life depends upon it. These are the *essential* elements of your new life. What's more, the new you, who is you combined with Jesus in you, actually wants to be doing them. You will never be healed and made whole without them. There's only one problem: Basic discipleship *alone* probably won't be enough to heal you. If it could then the whole church would be full of genuinely happy, emotionally healthy people who simply radiate the love and joy of the Lord. But that's hardly the way it is.

If the Body of Christ is an army, then let us acknowledge that every army nowadays has mobile hospital units for the necessary task of putting soldiers back together. As it is, we Christians are notorious for "shooting our wounded," heaping condemnation rather than grace upon those who can't march in ranks with the rest. Truth be told, most of our raw recruits need in-depth healing before being sent off to boot camp for basic training. I have seen so many well-intentioned new believers charge into the frontlines, spurred on by their comrades who mistake their zeal for maturity, only to be shot down and side-lined because they had no idea how to mend or tend their hearts. That is why this testimony of new life is leading into an extended section on healing—too many people have sold the idea that all you need is Jesus and everything will be fine. Yes, all you will ever need *is* Jesus, but you will need all He brings with Him to become complete, which includes both basic discipleship *and* emotional healing.

Believers with emotional wounds have a very hard time maintaining enough basic discipleship to stay "in the game." Once they lose their joy and their "first love"—their early enthusiasm and devotion to the Lord—they often also lose their zeal for sharing with others, their willingness to lay their lives down and their "hot" pursuit of Christ. Pretty soon it's all they can do just to show up at church, participate in a few functions and try not to lose more ground. Rather than thriving, they are merely surviving. Don't believe me? Just ask around: Almost everyone will say, "I'm hanging in there." That's certainly better than quitting, but it is not the goal! Holding on for dear life and toughing it out will keep you on the team, but you're still spending most of your time on the bench, rather than playing the game. Joyless Christianity is not the kind of life for which Jesus died to bring us. It's definitely not the kind of living that will attract non-believers to Christ: "Hey, want to know my Jesus and 'hang in there' with me?" "No thanks, I'm already doing that without Him. Why give up my freedom and the few pleasures I have left?"

The elements of basic discipleship I listed above are a vital portion of the new life, but you cannot coax or cajole people into taking them up if their hearts and lives are badly broken. I believe that we have only "slightly" healed the hurt of God's people (Jeremiah 8:11). This has contributed to the sad condition in the United States of a Christianity which is, as one visiting African bishop reportedly said, "An ocean that covers the continent, but is only one inch deep." We have not bridged the gap between the head and the heart. We have focused upon instructing the intellect but have greatly neglected training people in the way of the heart, and that necessarily includes healing emotional wounds so that genuine wholeness can be restored.

We may not apply it ourselves, but the enemy certainly seems to have taken the Word of the Lord, concerning our hearts, as a truth; his kingdom has targeted us where the most damage can be inflicted. Proverbs 3:24 says, "Keep your heart with all diligence for out of it spring the issues of life." Whose job is it to keep our hearts with all diligence? It is ours—"keep *your* heart." It evidently requires "all" diligence, which indicates that this necessary task cannot be fulfilled without intense and intentional effort on our part. In practical terms, guarding our heart means keeping it cleansed, open and held up to the Lord by a living faith so that His love, peace and joy keep flowing into us no matter what we are going through. We were all issued hearts both at birth and at the new birth. How few of us have been taught God's ways of "keeping" them!

This neglect of the heart greatly hinders us, for what is tucked away in our hearts holds the key to who we really are (Proverbs 23:7; 27:19). According to Jesus, our heart is also the wellspring for all of our words and actions, even the sinful ones (Matthew 15:18-19). I can honestly say that as a pastor, I have seen far more people overthrown by what was left un-mended in their hearts, than by wrong doctrine left unchecked in their minds. Thankfully, the Spirit of the Lord brought this to my attention early. From the beginning of my new life in Christ I was asking God fervently and frequently to "lead me in a path with a heart." I didn't want to end up with an intellectually correct faith and an unsatisfied and un-ravished heart! I didn't want to talk about God's love and not *be* love. I wanted His way of peace to become a river of life in me 24/7—not just something to touch base with on Sundays.

For that to happen, God had a lot of mending to do. The heart works by the same rule as computers: *garbage in, garbage out.* Unless you and I work with the Lord to get the garbage out, the festering mess inside will spill out onto the people around us and, frankly, make life odious for us as well. Since I had nailed my tongue and my actions to the cross, I knew I had to get the Lord to sort out my insides or stuff was going to explode some point down the road. That and being only too aware of the emotional pain I carried with me daily, launched me on a journey to find healing. What I learned on that journey became the basis of our healing ministry.

Damage Assessment

One of the things the Holy Spirit helps us with is assessing the damage. This takes thoughtful observation because to our unschooled way of thinking, ongoing damage may seem to be the enemy's work through and through. Like water seeking a leak, the enemy searches out all of our wrongheaded thinking and wounded emotions to hit us where it hurts or uses temptation to gain access to our will where we are weakest. Nevertheless, the Holy Spirit works through these attacks to show us where the damage lies. Many of us have buried the sources of our emotional pain, spending a fair amount of both mental and emotional energy and effort to keep them "under wraps." Almost all of the coping strategies we come up with are things of the carnal nature that must be abandoned if our true life is ever to emerge. If we are not careful, we may use basic discipleship like a lawn mower to keep the weeds down instead of pulling them up by the roots. We need inner healing to get at the roots. Take it as gospel that wherever there is bad fruit there is a root that has been feeding it (Matthew 7:17; Hebrews 12:15). At the beginning of my walk I was mowing down weeds constantly!

As it happened I didn't come into awareness of every area in my life that needed healing all at once. I'm sure no one could handle it, even if they could be shown all areas. I'm also sure that I'm still being mended as I go along—heaven alone provides the final cure. But I will list my main roots and weeds so that you can see and perhaps relate to at least some of the issues. In the remainder of this section I will be showing you how the Lord brought me healing. He won't do it in exactly the same way for you, but He will work through many of the same methods and by means of many of the same truths. People say that His ways are strange. They're not. They make perfect sense once you have the advantage of hindsight. It's *we* who are strange. We are the ones who don't live by trusting ourselves to His truth, love and mercy; therefore, we need a lot of convincing that His ways really do work.

Here's the laundry list of my strange ways:

1) Shyness: Practically the first thing I noticed that needed fixing was that I was so incredibly shy. I had no comfort level around anyone except June, not even with our kids one-on-one. Deep down I was fearful of everyone and very nervous in group settings, especially if I had to speak. Yet, I was convinced I was called to preach. This motivated me to get it mended.

2) Hurts from Others: The night of my conversion I blurted out to the Lord, "I want everyone who ever hurt me forgiven!" Right away, I started discovering just how many and how deep were the wounds collected from childhood. If the heart is meant to be like an open hand to others, mine was a fist hold-

ing on to every past wrong. The motivation to be healed of this was weak at best.

3) Self-Hatred: I hated myself! I was so angry with myself that I would have spit in my face if the wind was right. I couldn't get over how much hell I had literally put myself through. I kept myself under "house arrest," always coming down hard on myself for even the slightest infractions. I didn't feel like I was a human being, and I hated myself for it. How *could* this be fixed?

4) Feeling Rejected: No one could love me, or so I was convinced. My past was bad enough, but even my present would run people off if they only knew me better. I was still wounded by the massive rejection I endured by the god who sent me into hell and by all the imagined rejections of others.

5) Grieving the Losses: My "soggy heart" was a part of me that was brimful of tears that I had never shed in grief over people I had lost along the way. This was a heavy, hurting weight I didn't want touched by me or anyone else. Not even by God.

6) The Father Wound: This felt like a sharp pain lodged in my heart. I did not feel that I had ever bonded with my own father, and I was terrified at the thought of Father God losing patience with me. I feared Him, not in a good way.

7) The Occult Legacy: There were shadowy sides of me that seemed ghostlike and unreal. There was a deep fear of going back into the delusion again; the true sighting of hell I had glimpsed seared me. Perversely, I became angry with the God who saved me, but hadn't spared me, from hell on earth.

That's not all, but it includes the major pieces of my brokenness. I hope my list gives you hope for your own healing if you are one who needs it. Someone once said that Jesus can mend your broken heart, but you have to give Him *all* the pieces. It's quite a puzzle from our perspective, but He's already had millenniums of experience working with others. He comes to us with an excellent track record as the best Puzzle Solver out there. I have often joked that the thing which qualifies me for leading a healing ministry is that I was so badly broken by my fall that only a great God could put me back together. I simply took notes on how He did it. Those notes became whole sections in our Healing Streams workbook.

Damage assessment should also include what survived the crisis—the things you can count on that are still working. In addition to having kept my family together and giving me a business to run, the Lord got me started with a truckload of mending that first night. That was a huge advantage! It really, really helps to know Him, to know His Word is truth, to have His Spirit living in you, to be a part of His Body on earth, and to have your sins forgiven. There's much more to our inheritance in Christ, but almost everyone knows that the big five I just listed are part of their "starter kit." We never grow out of these truths by the way, we keep growing *into them,* and as we do, a whole lot of liberation comes our way. Everyone who receives faith in Jesus gets this same starter kit. Few, however, are fully mended by these five things alone.

I was also liberated by being set free from seven demons, from classic paranoia, from schizophrenia, from the delusion of hell, from an addiction to pornography and from a handful of illnesses. All of this had happened in less than an hour. It amazes me that so many Christians head out to the secular world for their mental and emotional healing. Perhaps we do not know how much is available to us; perhaps it's not readily available in our area. I have to admit that I didn't know what was actually available in terms of Christian ministries, only that I was convinced that God was going to heal me *in every way* and that He would be using His own methods and His own believing people to do it.

To make things easier for you to track along with me on this journey I have numbered the following chapters to match my list of wounds. They are not in sequential order, so you can jump ahead to read up on ones that may match your particular needs or simply take them as they come. My main purpose in setting these areas of healing before you is so that you can see ways that you, too, can bring your own heart to God for healing, if you need it, or help the ones around you who may be wounded in these ways.

Shyness (1)

The hardest thing to get about shyness, if you want to be free of it, is that it is a sin. Wait a minute. Isn't it a personality disorder, a psychological problem? Of course it is. Sin is what *dis*-orders the personality that God actually gives us; sin is what causes problems in our psychological, emotional and spiritual make-up. God fashions us in the womb in *His Image*. He doesn't put sinful or fallen things on us. The enemy does that through Adam's sin (the original sin), through generational sin, through the sins of others and through our own sinful reactions. Since I had been shy as long as I had known myself, it took me a year or so to comprehend this. Roy Hessian's little book, *Calvary Road*, brought this understanding home to me, but I was already groping towards it. Instinctively, we all want to be free. I haven't met a shy person yet who really wanted to *be* shy. I felt trapped, like a person in a glass house, behind a wall of insecurity and inferiority. I wanted desperately to be able to go out and play with the other kids in my new neighborhood!

Since my determination to struggle towards freedom was so great, most of the time I refused to back away from doing things just because my shy side was acting up. I challenged my fears on purpose. I did lots of things afraid and that simple virtue of persistence began to build a fragile sense of confidence that I could survive in a world of people. You don't have to be a believer in anything but yourself to do this. In high school I had won public speaking awards, been in plays and in the public eye, all without losing one teensy bit of shyness. The new piece of divine equipping, however, was that it really helps if you become a believer in *the Lord's ability*, rather than just your own, to help you manage your shyness. You can then grow a greater confidence in God, which will help you overcome all kinds of fears.

Once you can confess shyness as a sin, you begin to get more lasting victories for two reasons: It invites God to work where the problem really lies; it also leads to a radical re-envisioning of who you actually are. First, the problem is not "out there" in the scary world of people and the risky life of faith, it is "in here"—in a heart that chooses not to trust God with your very life. This has to be named and confessed as sin because it is sin. Once that's accomplished, you and God can be "on the same page" in working with the real problem. Second, you are not shy. If you have Jesus in you, then you are united *at the core of your being* with the least shy Person in the universe. You have been made one with Him; His nature is now in you. He says His redeemed are "bold as lions" (Proverbs 28:1). That's because He knows who we really are. He knows what is in the new heart and spirit He has put inside of us. He knows what we are capable of becoming once we put our trust *entirely* in Him.

Often by using others, what the enemy puts in through his own sins against us is the fear of man, people pleasing, and pride, an inordinate self-focus. I know now that what comes in can also go out. Knowing and naming what needs to be dispensed of as sin strengthens our resolve not to let it hamper whatever the Lord may be asking of us. If you think you are fighting against your own innate personality, then good luck. How can self defeat Self? That's a guaranteed formula for discouragement. It made all the difference in the world to see that the truth about myself is that, at heart, I already am a person who loves and enjoys the company of others. In this way I was much more able to resist shyness, relax and focus on others. Such trust and shift of focus from oneself then allows the Holy Spirit to bring forth the new nature that God has already placed inside of us. It was a long time coming, but nobody who knows me now believes I ever had a shy side.

Even so the enemy completely hoodwinked me concerning the fear of speaking in public, a sin that is closely related to shyness. When I arrived at Christ Church fresh out of seminary I was petrified of the pulpit. This went on for years. Just trying to study the scriptures for an assignment would induce a hyperventilating, heart-pounding, cross-eyed, brain-fogged sorry state of affairs. You would think that God would give you more confidence if He was calling you to preach. Fears, however, tell us a lot more about ourselves, than they do about what God's will for us may be. I have found that God often calls us to walk in the direction of our fears. Lacking any better answer, I preached afraid for years. Eventually as my preaching got better, my confidence in God rose and my fear diminished. Once again, though, what gave me the final victory was confessing fear of speaking in public as sin, just as I had done with shyness years earlier. Why I didn't get that revelation sooner, I don't know, but it definitely brought greater freedom once I began applying it in earnest.

Hurts from Others (2)

Forgiving others was a lesson I was doggedly trying to apply right from the beginning. Unfortunately, I didn't know how to do it, so I kept fumbling around with prayers that probably were going in the right direction but weren't moving much freight. I was also going round and round the mountains that needed moving looking for excuses. I knew almost instinctively that forgiveness was a good principle—I had embraced it *in general* the night of my conversion—but I kept imagining that there were exceptions, especially in my case. There was also confusion in the Body of Christ surrounding me about forgiveness and that added to mine. People would say, what I now realize are totally erroneous things, like, "Sure God can forgive, but He's God—I can't," or, "I can forgive, but I'll never get over it," or, "I forgave, but I can't forget," or (my personal favorite), "I've forgiven him and I love him with the love of Jesus, but I sure don't like him." You've probably heard them too. Maybe even thought them yourself. I know I did.

What really helped me, oddly enough, was a situation that came about where I absolutely could not go on with my cherished dream of becoming a priest unless I forgave someone who stood in the way. This person didn't know the hurt I carried and the injustice I felt over his actions against me—but I did. What made it worse was that I knew God knew about my hardened heart too. He was telling me He wouldn't be able to use me like He would like to in ministry, unless I learned how to forgive people *from the heart*. I learned through this that situations where we feel aggrieved, where the other person is offering us no satisfaction in terms of repentance or apology or restitution can be an absolute godsend. I don't believe for one minute that God causes bad things to happen, or in any way desires them, but He can make good use of any bad thing we bring to Him and best use of the worst things we bring to Him. Although it took me at least a year, once I finally forgave him my heart resurfaced into the relationship. I not only recovered the friendship, I also gained this person as an ally towards seminary. This was an important early victory at growing a forgiving heart, and it showed me the direction I would need to go to receive major healing in the future.

Forgiveness is the coin of the realm where the life and power of God's Kingdom are concerned. It is perhaps the chief thing that we love about Jesus, for He gave this to us by the death He suffered. Not only that but it forms the basis for how God relates to us through the New Covenant; it is how He desires us to relate to *all* others, and it is also how we want others to relate to us. The Father completely cleared His own great heart towards us at the cross and fully expects us to learn how to do the same. I knew these things from the beginning. Yet despite the knowledge, this was a lesson that came, well, very *grudgingly* into my actual practice.

I say this to my shame, but I had a very hard time releasing my father from accumulated hurts—and he was a good father. What made it difficult I think was that I didn't actually bond with him until just before he died, when we spent a long week-end together telling each other all the many stories of our lives that we had never shared. Some months prior to that weekend I had completely forgiven him and perhaps God used the grace of that to release something in us both. I had forgiven him while I was at a church camp reading Gordon Dalbey's *Father and Son: the Wound, the Healing, the Call to Manhood.* Through it I realized that my dad, too, was the wounded son of an imper-fect father. Something very hurt and very hard in my heart completely gave way. As it did I had the strangest sensation. I looked up to the Lord and said, "Here I am, a pickup truck driving former hippie carpenter, who my wife thinks is a secret redneck and yet, for the first time in my life I feel like a real man. What's going on?" He said, "Until this moment you were a boy trying to be a man." That was two healings for the price of one! By forgiving my father and completely accepting him in that role, I was not only freed of my pain, I was also no longer rejecting my life as his son. Nor was I any longer, unconscious-ly, rejecting the Father in heaven who had chosen my earthly father. These things are so deep that only the Holy Spirit can search them out for us. Thank God He does.

A few months later I cashed in on a bumper crop of mercy. It happened one day while I was in my office at Christ Church. I was going over my litany of all the men in authority who had broken my trust or wounded me with injustice from childhood to the present. It was quite a list. Like a swarm of bees the names, faces and events kept coming after me, no matter what I did to try to release them. *Why me? Why couldn't men in authori-ty treat me right?* I stood up, walked into a corner, turned to face the Lord and said not very politely, "You've backed me into a corner with this. There's going to be no way into the life I want unless I fully forgive them from the heart, is there?"

It was at that moment that I saw it: the sin of my own unforgiveness. I fell to my knees in deep repentance and cried out for mercy—mercy not to walk away with, but mercy with which to do the forgiving. In my mind's eye I saw all my "assailants" also kneeling at the cross beside me, seeking mercy. I said to them, "Fellows, don't worry about it. It's no longer about what you did to me, it's about what I've been doing to you and to Jesus—*in my own heart.*" Then I turned to the Lord and said, "Jesus, by not forgiving them I have been sinning against You every waking moment of my life. Forgive me as I forgive them." When I stood up from that time of letting go, I felt entirely free, even invincible. I told the Lord that this day He had given me a "Teflon-coated heart." It was not the heart I wanted—I wanted a heart that couldn't be wounded—but it was a heart that had just learned how to *fully* forgive and because of that no hurt could ever stick to me again. Even better than the healing has been that "Teflon-coated equipping," since being wounded by people goes hand-in-hand with loving with them. Learning to fully forgive from the heart is tremendous equipping for *life!*

Self-Hatred (3)

The hardest person of all to forgive is the one who has caused the deepest and most enduring injury and pain. In my life that was me. No one else even came close to the damage levels I had initiated. What made things worse was that I was still the source of my own undoing by a steady stream of sins, stupidities and weaknesses. There was no end in sight! It was as if God wanted to teach me how to "love the sinner and hate the sin" by assigning me to myself as the worst scoundrel in Christendom. I would have to learn how to love and forgive myself. Me, the would-be lover of Jesus and Christian saint, was joined at the hip with me, the sorry sinner. "Stevie Wonder" was still wrecking my life! This greatly reinforced the warrant I had issued against myself as Public Enemy Number One during those ten years in hell. With each new transgression I bound myself with fresh chains: Self-hatred was the jailor. I despaired of ever getting any better.

I had no idea what a blessing this was! Until we lose all hope for finding refuge and rescue through Self, we do not fully turn to Jesus and cast all our hope on Him alone. We keep trying to get Self — that false god — to work for us, and Self will never be a sufficient savior for anyone's life. What tripped me up was that I thought I had fully done this the night I asked Jesus to be my Savior. Indeed, I was delighted to know that He was not only saving me from my hell, but also from the true hell; He was saving me *for* eternity in heaven as well. How good is that? I had once been blind, but now I could see the light. What I didn't see was how I had become "blinded" by that light into thinking I had surrendered *all* to Jesus. In reality I was feverishly trying to get Self (myself), rather than Jesus, to save me in countless other ways. In His wisdom God had to allow Self to keep crashing to the ground, otherwise I would have all too willingly and unwittingly built my life around the counterfeit trinity: me, myself and I.

Not having the benefit of any of this more seasoned perspective, I was scared witless that my repeated failures would eventually bring great wrath upon me. But truth be known, I was terrified at the thought of even *minor* wrath. I couldn't bear the idea that I was using up my allotment of grace and that *this* God would eventually realize that I was a hopeless case, casting me aside just as the other god had. So I redoubled my efforts which only increased my failures! Years down the road, the words of François Fénelon came to me like a cool breeze blowing through my desert, "Expect nothing of yourself, but all things of God. Knowledge of our own hopeless, incorrigible weakness, with unreserved confidence in God's power, are the true foundations of all spiritual life."[5] God was building the foundation, but it sure didn't look like it at the time. All I could see was the ruin of Self.

Old habits are hard to change. Since I was so "unfixable," hating myself had become deeply ingrained as the obvious answer to the problem of me being me. I never questioned this mental habit and it reigned supreme. Unlike our fears, I have noticed that the Lord doesn't always go directly at a stronghold—our mental blocks are too well-fortified against rational argument—but undermines them in order to bring them down or distracts us in order to gain entry. He came at me sideways. He recruited me quite easily into a program of seeking to become judgment-free with everyone I met. I had seen how He loves and accepts people just as they are and I wanted to be like that. After a year or so of this training, He tapped me on the shoulder one day and said, *You know how you've been trying to show unconditional acceptance to people I bring you for ministry?* "Yeah, I'm glad you noticed. So, You think I'm doing OK?" *I'd like you to be that way with yourself.* "What? How can I? Really? You mean I could?" This was divine permission to treat myself as I was trying to treat others, a graceful inversion of the Golden Rule. The "sneaky" God had worked around me!

I really liked the idea once I got hold of it, but changing this habit was like trying to stop a speeding locomotive on a downhill run. Then there was shock therapy. One time He played back to me a mental soundtrack of how I had actually been talking to myself—berating myself in my thoughts in ways I would never have dreamed of speaking out loud to others. That jolted me into a fair bit of recognition. He also gave me a vision in which I was holding a replica of myself: my left arm gripping my back and shoulders and with my right hand just pounding away on my face. While I was doing this I was looking up to God and saying, "See? You don't have to punish me.

---

[5] François Fénelon, *Spiritual Letters to Women* (New Canaan, Connecticut: Keats Publishing, Inc., 1980). p. 55.

I'm doing it for You!" These "reality checks" truly startled me and helped me see truth. Truth, however, is sometimes like a mountain in the distance. Once you see it, you might decide to climb it, but it still takes a long time and a lot of effort to get to the top.

One of the foothills along the way to climbing that mountain came about ten years into my walk. I had been having trouble with something I called the "Bear Trap." It had been in me all along, but it wasn't until seminary that I was actually able to separate it from all the other stuff, to identify it as a specific problem and give it a name. Identifying and naming problems helps you manage them without the panic of not knowing what *in blazes* is going on. It also helps you explain it to someone else. At one point I was explaining the "Bear Trap" to a Christian psychologist I had been seeing for a year. I told him that there was something going on inside me that felt exactly like my entire chest and guts would get caught by an emotional bear trap whenever I did something wrong real or imagined, and that it would take days before I could get free of the intense pain. After the pain passed, that freedom would only last for a day at the most before something else triggered the emotional mechanism. He told me I would have to learn to live with it. I went for a second opinion.

In only one morning of ministry, Don and Ann Block of Jacksonville, Florida, very quickly identified the root problems as inner vows and bitter judgments that I had made against myself during the years in hell. All of the self-cursing from those days had to be repented and renounced. They broke the curse, and the "Bear Trap" was cast off. It has never returned! As I rode home to Savannah that afternoon the Lord provided the most spectacular, longest lasting rainbow I have ever seen stretching over the exact direction I was travelling. I thought that meant I was in the homestretch in terms of my healing— wishful thinking. It turned out that there would be another ten years to the journey, and I was only halfway home. I'm very sure, however, that the rainbow meant Jesus was rejoicing with me that the big, bad "Bear Trap" was dead.

Another major foothill then appeared on the horizon. I was reading books on healing and learning a lot about the power of words and of our inner beliefs. You would think that the words beaten into a child by an unloving person would be words he/she would throw off as quickly as possible. Sadly, this is not the case. Children take things to heart, especially if a parent speaks them. Just as deadly, they can add their own words or wrong interpretive conclusions: "There must be something wrong with me, look how I'm being treated; No one loves me; I should never have been born." In all of this there is an invisible enemy secretly "fathering" us by planting his twisted words, though they are disguised as our own thoughts. With me it wasn't words from my earliest years that got stuck inside, but words from those years in hell. The trick is catching these little foxes that spoil the vine—they are so *ingrained* they go unnoticed and unquestioned, like the pattern of the wood that may be in the reading table beside you.

One night I intentionally hunkered down near the most hurting place in my heart and despite my tears was listening for whatever I might hear. A tiny little voice seemed to be crying, "No one could love me. I can't be loved. I can't love me." *Aha! I've got you!* I exclaimed as I seized that thought and carried it captive to Christ. It took some doing because so much of me was in emotional agreement with those ideas, but I managed to fully and deeply renounce them as not being true and instead chose to believe that I *could be loved* and *am loved* now that Jesus is in my life. This breakthrough needed to happen or I could never have advanced to the mountain I really wanted to climb, the one that held the towering perspective of seeing myself as God sees me—with unconditional acceptance.

About a year or so later I was nearing the summit but didn't know it. It can be like that in the mountains if you get caught in a whiteout from fog or cloud—you lose your sense of perspective and position. In the spiritual life clouds represent God (they float down from heaven); fog represents confusion (it rises up from the earth). The first Mystery delights us; the second thwarts us. I often don't know which is which when my vision is reduced. You just have to grope your way along and try not to lose your footing. This particular night, as so often happened, I was caught in a tight crevasse between the proverbial rock and the hard place. I had come down very hard on myself about something and had begun actively hating myself, but I knew that my heavenly Rock didn't want me being that way.

Searching in the Spirit for a handhold on some kind of truth that would help me climb out, I said to myself at last, "OK, I'll forgive you once more, but you just better not mess up again." *I don't want you doing it that way—that's conditional forgiveness.* "It's the best I can do," I quickly retorted, but His words forced me to realize that this was all I had ever done: let myself off the hook on the impossible condition that I had better never goof up again or else. "What more can I do? I *never* get any better! It is so frustrating!" *Forgive yourself once and for all totally without conditions as a gift to Me. Then I want you to confess from your heart that it's a great, good thing to be you.* I lost it. I laughed, but it wasn't a pretty laugh; I then fired back, "How can that possibly be true? Here I am still carrying so much pain from the past, still dealing with so much wreck and ruin, still so far from entering into my real calling, still so completely messed up. And I'm not getting any younger!"

Sometimes God has to read you the riot act. There really was a Riot Act in pre-Victorian England, which officials would read to unruly crowds before dismissing them from soccer matches that ended in brawls or political rallies that smacked of rebellion. In my rebellion, I was close to brawling with God. He, on the other hand, was reciting to me with the patience of a true Father a list of reasons from His perspective: *It's a great, good thing to be you, because I will always be forgiving you and loving you no matter how badly you are doing, I will never reject you or forsake you, I am eager to save you and come whenever you call, I am always making good plans for you, and I am totally committed to bringing good out of anything you mess up or any evil done to you.* Silence. A very big piece fell softly into place. "Well, since you put it like that, I have to say that it really is a great, good thing to be me, but *only* because I have You for my God!" Just like that I came out of years of self-hatred and into unspeakable joy, filled full with glory. Self had finally been overthrown! It really is a great, good thing to be the one He loves, even if it means being me just as I am or you just as you are.

It didn't last long though. I stumbled over some small mistake the next day, got furious with myself and lost the inward blessing of *feeling* so completely accepting of myself and desiring of my life. This tied me up in such a knot—*how could I have lost that blessing!* It was a full year before I could find it in my heart to say those same things again and sufficiently believe them to be set free, though I tried practically every day to get those feelings back. When it happened at last, the joy and sense of glory returned. But I lost it, once again, the next day over a trifle. That time it took nine months to get it back. I lost it again the very next day. Six months of struggle ensued before restoration. Finally, I caught on to something. I thought to myself, "Wait a minute. Instead of focusing on what I lost and being angry, I should focus on getting it back. Instead of demanding that I never lose the feeling and being angry, my goal should be a quicker recovery of believing the truths that produced the feeling in the first place." This new strategy worked like a champ! In retrospect I know that it was heaven-sent, even though it came into my mind disguised as my own thoughts. Now I almost never lose the feeling. But when I do, it's easy as pie to get it back. That's the beauty of learning how to believe truth. Feelings will always spring up out of what we deeply believe—you can't change that. But you can change what you believe to be true. Real truth, God's truth, will always liberate your feelings once you believe it *from the heart.*

Feeling Rejected (4)

Feelings of rejection can be compared to a ten ton gorilla that likes nothing better than to sit on you. I'll take the gorilla every time! Nobody I know likes feeling rejected; it feels so terrible. Most people I know have a coping strategy for rejection. Some strategies work better than others; some are more socially acceptable. I had several which began in childhood: hiding out in shyness as I withdrew from possible rejection like a turtle into his shell; escaping into fantasy where I lived in dreams of a me that others would admire and never reject; seething and sulking in repressed anger, planning ways of getting even; and scrambling up the ladder of achievement to get my cup filled with "attaboys" instead of putdowns. By early adulthood some of these coping mechanisms were operating at industrial strength. For instance, although I never let anyone know it because they might have rejected me for it, I kept a Gatling gun inside me that found fault with everyone I met. That way their opinion wouldn't matter to me if it ever went against me.

There's a saying, "What goes around, comes around." Rejection operates by this principle, but it certainly is no merry-go-round in terms of being a fun ride. Because of the injustice and pain of rejection received, we may become rejecters of others. In learning to form judgments against others, it becomes possible to form judgments against ourselves and reject ourselves. This happens if we start agreeing with others' rejection of us or turn against ourselves because we can't find a way to avoid being someone people reject. In point of hard fact, rejection is impossible to avoid. Even Jesus couldn't avoid it and He was perfect! Being far from perfect I did a lot that was rejection worthy. I also speeded up the merry-go-round by rejecting others and rejecting myself. This hypersensitizes us to being hurt by imagining future rejections from others or thinking we've been rejected where none was intended. Round and round we go.

In the beginning, I never imagined that God would ever reject me—I was the hero of my story. Surely I would be vindicated in the end. However, once I rejected the true God, the day came when my newfound god indeed rejected me. That was perhaps the only truth the "god of this world" showed me— Satan hates and rejects us. He will never turn from his fierce judgments against us. This rejection, because it seemed so cosmic and absolute, seared me completely. My own self-rejection reached its apex as I entered into total agreement with my god's final judgment and eternal condemnation of me. Damnation is *deserved* rejection for which there can be no remedy. It stung me to the core.

Isn't this, in a sense, what we all fear? It is not actual death, but rather "the sting of death" which is sin (1 Corinthians 15:56). Who knows, we might die, and it may turn out to be not so bad? Perhaps we will awaken to cosmic bliss, another shot at life, or simply drift off into the Big Sleep. But sin *stings us* with the painful truth that there will be a judgment to face, a judgment that no one is able to face without a Savior from sin. Isn't this what rejection by others plays into? The terrible, secret knowledge that there is Something Wrong going on deep inside, the wrong of original sin. We may not know ourselves as sinners in rebellion against our God, but we do know that we don't *know* Him like we should. We know that we are not the person we should be. We know that there is something we have lost and cannot recover, the original innocence. Ultimately, we know one day we will have to face Him, and that we won't be able to give sufficient answer when we do. The rejections of other people draws its strength from this secret knowledge— secret only because we half-hide it from ourselves. If people reject me, might not the ultimate Person reject me? I had to live with *that* rejection for ten years, not as guesswork but as punishing, uncompromising fact. This left me with guilt-ridden feelings from past rejection and anxious fears of future rejection. Fearing rejection doesn't help. If only it did, I would have been home free.

Being a new Christian naturally brought my Doo Bee side out with flying colors. Of course I wanted to be good and to do right. That was genuine, but it wasn't the whole story. I didn't want to give God or anyone else a target to shoot at! Good luck. The math for keeping score on rejection is stacked against us — ten hard-won affirmations can be wiped out in an instant by a single off-handed rejection. Additionally, most of us have a backlog from the past. I carried rejection wounds from friends who betrayed me, from bullies who tormented me, from girls who jilted me. These were slight compared to everything else, but they had been the seedbed out of which the infernal vine had grown. It turned out I was still smarting from having been asked to leave choir in the sixth grade. The teacher had been very kind — it was a mercy killing and I even knew it at the time. I really couldn't sing and it embarrassed me to have to try. The thing is that it embarrassed me even more to be asked *not* to try; I was so thin-skinned. Thank God my heart is free of all this at last!

How did it happen? How was freedom won? In every case I had to forgive the person who rejected me, whether real or imagined and put away those hard feelings. That thorn had to be completely removed and replaced with positive feelings for the offender. Then I had to find a way to give the hurt feelings to God. It helped to look toward something good I might have learned or some way in which I might have grown. This was putting Romans 8:28 to work: "We know that for those who love God all things work together for good." Slowly coming to see that this promise was true in some instances enabled me to embrace it as an invariable rule in all cases. After a while I no longer needed to look for something redemptive about the experience of rejection, past or present, I just *knew* it was there. This was beginning to work most of the time.

What worked even better was using each instance of felt or remembered rejection as an opportunity to believe truth at a depth level. I would vigorously rehearse to my wounded heart truths from scripture that I had not known when past rejections occurred or still didn't know well enough to protect me with God's armor in the present. Truth is far better protection than walls, but you have to believe truth *from the heart* for it to be effective. When Nehemiah had the assignment of rebuilding the ruined walls of Jerusalem, he ordered half the people to work with their swords and spears at the ready, for the enemy might attack at any moment, while the others hoisted the burned stones into place, which were painful reminders of past attacks. We build our new walls of protection, not with hard feelings but with truths; yet, we are building while still under attack and often by working with painful memories from the past in order to "fit" them into the new framework of Christian truth. The truths I was building with were "God has accepted me in Christ; God loves me as I am; God wants everyone to love me too; even I can love me. This has always been true. It will always be true." *Repeat as needed.*

All of this good training fell apart at a later date in my life, when it seemed that several people had rejected me without cause and were spreading rumors and falsehood. Most days I love what Mother Teresa wrote: "Why worry what others are saying about you? Suppose they knew the truth." The truth is I may not have been guilty of those accusations, but *I am rejection worthy*—I deserved to die on that cross, not Jesus. However, I failed to see any humor in what I was going through at the time. I began complaining strenuously to the Lord, "I'm going to forgive them, but You just don't know how much it hurts!" Now that's comical—telling Jesus, who was put to death by His own people, that He doesn't know how much rejection can hurt a guy! I sensed the irony of it, but pursued my complaint just the same. Then I became suddenly aware of a Presence.

Jesus was standing right behind me and a bit off to my left. I couldn't see Him with my eyes, but His Hands were outstretched with palms up, and He was saying to me with a twinkle of humor, "So what am I to you, Steve? Chopped liver?" The Jewish delicatessen flavor to His question really cracked me up! I broke out laughing, "Yes, I'm sure You're right Lord. What was I thinking? You're the only one who ever died for me. You're always with me, loving me. You matter more than anyone else possibly could." Then I got it. "Oh, My God! I've got a bigger problem than I thought!"

In fact I had two problems. Rejection keeps you looking at what others did or said, as if that were your real problem. It never wants you looking at what you are doing or saying. Holding on to rejection is a *double* sin: It is the sin of idolatry of others because it puts their opinion of you above God's; and it is the sin of unbelief because you believe what your feelings are telling you, rather than what God has declared in His Word. Now check me on this: What was the chart topping sin on God's list of ten things *never* to do? Idolatry (Exodus 20:3). And what was the sin that barred the way of the Israelites into the Promised Land? Unbelief (Hebrews 3:19). Holding on to feelings of rejection had me sinning—without realizing it—in two very major ways.

Let's pause for a principle: All sin separates us from God, but not all sins are equal in their effects. Some sins have a small effect in us or on others (little "white lies" for instance); some have a more hurtful effect on others (adultery, murder); and some have a very hurtful effect *in us* (rejection for example). The power of the pain usually indicates the gravity of the disease. Holding on to feelings of rejection *really* hurts. It is a deadly *dis*-ease of the soul that needs a powerful remedy.

Immediately, I went to the Lord in prayer, confessing and thoroughly repenting of all my previous agreements with these two sins; I had Him pull my heart out of other people and plug it into Him. As I chose to believe the truth *with all my heart* that

He has unfailing love and acceptance for me, I felt my heart's need for acceptance come to rest in His own great Heart like a ship held secure in a safe harbor. The Father's total acceptance of us in the Beloved is the true antidote for every instance of rejection (Ephesians 1:6). As I let that greater truth wash over me, all past and present feelings of rejection and fears of rejection fell away. Then I asked Him to let me be "burned as needed" if I started touching "the hot stove" of idolatry of other people's opinions again. Sometimes you have to apply iodine to the wound to be sure of the healing. The wound of rejection got healed that day. It has remained well healed ever since!

Grieving the Losses (5)

It seems that we have a spiritual anatomy that somehow mirrors our physical anatomy. Scripture speaks of the heart and mind of the New Creation, and Paul plays out this analogy fairly extensively in terms of the corporate Body of Christ. I don't want to press the image too far, but I became aware of my spiritual anatomy through recognition that grief was actually lodged in a very specific location in my physical body. Due to its location I called it my "soggy heart." Of course I never spoke of this out loud—I wasn't about to let anyone pry it open with words. I didn't even want God to touch it. So, I kept it sealed up, but always in the back of my mind I was aware of heaviness, a deep unanswered sorrow that radiated from a part of my heart, which I knew to be filled with tears.

I was only too well aware of how I got saddled with this soggy heart. It dated back to the time I was desperately trying to keep my life from going down the drain. This lasted for a full year and a half, until the Night of Terror finally arrived and hell ended all thought of rescue. During this period I was filled with the conviction that the lives of everyone I knew and cared about were connected to mine by this same universal spirit through which I was seeking transformation. As I grew increasingly delusional, I lost my normal life connections with all of them, which grieved me tremendously. But it was much worse than that due to the deception: I entirely believed, rather I was *made* to believe, that they had died when I "died." I was responsible for the death of everyone I loved! This brought such grief and guilt upon me that I might have been swallowed by it alone, had not the terrors of hell been a more profound and pressing problem.

Now that I was out of the delusion, the grief and guilt that I had shoved down years before were trying to resurface, seeking to be heard. My response? Not on your life—*I'm not listening!* This became so engrafted that if my soggy heart ever began to surface during an unguarded moment, I would slam-dunk it by a practiced inward reflex. Meanwhile "sneaky" God was working to undermine this towering stronghold by another strategy. He was reacquainting me with tears and getting me to like them. Throughout the ten years of "burning" in hell I could not cry—would not cry—although I remember misting up once or twice watching a sad scene in a movie like *Casablanca*. I suppose that real tears need a modicum of hope that someone somewhere may hear our cry and listen, perhaps even bring help. I didn't have a shred of hope, so why bother? I am certain that in the real hell the damned are screaming for all they are worth, though that reality is too horrible for me to hold very long in thought. But I seriously doubt any of them are shedding tears—there is no one there who cares.

Now that I was saved and back on planet earth, the Lord had opened up whole rivers of tears within me. I could cry for joy over being alive again, for sorrow over sins and in compassion for the hurts of others. I would cry reading scripture. *Your truth is so beautiful!* I still do to this day, even when leading a service. Tears also flowed freely when the presence of the Lord drew near and whenever I was drawn into intercessory travail for the lost or for world calamities. And I was glad for it. At the very least, tears remind us "hardboiled" men that we have a heart after all. Tears soften the heart the way soft rain prepares the soil for planting. Never disparage tears poured out before God: They are liquid prayers. God *listens* to every drop. They matter to Him.

Tears must matter to Him because I can testify that the Lord seemed very determined to get me to open my soggy heart to His ministrations. It is comical in hindsight—He would touch me *there*, I would slam it down; He would touch me *there*, I would slam it down. Finally, I caught on. I realized He was after my secret stash of tears, so I decided to open up, to take a chance and get a conversation going. Are you aware that we can refuse to speak to Him; refuse to listen? He loves us enough to let us shut down, but it is ill advised. I said a bit testily, "What are You doing?" *I want you to give Me those tears.* "You don't understand. It's way too deep. If I start crying those tears I will *never* come to the end of them." *You don't understand. Tears are finite. My joy is infinite. Give Me the tears so you can enter My joy.* It was an offer I couldn't refuse.

I knew that I would never open this up around anyone else, but since I was already sitting in a comfortable chair and since there was no one at home at the time, I asked Him to help me get started by putting me in touch with the feelings. Wham! Suddenly, I could not stop crying. Great wracking sobs were streaming out of me. It was a torrent of pent-up tears. While it was passing through me the only conscious connection I could make to it was the general period of time I knew it involved. I prayed a bit in tongues, but mainly I just gave myself to the tears and imagined that Jesus was sitting opposite me, listening to my heart cry. He showed me that I could not cry when all of this happened to me because I would not allow myself to cry into an empty universe. Now everything was different—He was here comforting me with His presence.

After about twenty or thirty minutes of this unrestrained flood, I told Him that was all I could do and that I needed to take a break for the day, but I would come back to it the next day whenever He would arrange the time. We did this together every day or so for a month. Towards the end of the month, with no abatement to the volume or violence of the tears, I asked Him if I was anywhere near the end of it. *Soon.* "Soon? It seems to me You used that same word to describe Your return and it's been almost two thousand years!" *Soon.* Fortunately for me, *soon* came sooner rather than later. Much to my surprise, only a few days later I cried the last tear. In the ensuing silence, I got up, went into the kitchen and fixed a cup of tea. Then I took a good look inside my formerly soggy heart. It was entirely empty! There was no grief, no guilt, no heaviness left, only a quiet spring of joy bubbling gently up to the surface. *Lord, You did it all without words or prayers! You did it with the tears!* Take heart, dear reader. Give God your tears. Hold nothing back. There's joy on the other side of them.

The Father Wound (6)

The father wound is so intimately bound up with our self-image that the healing of one needs to go hand-in-hand with the healing of the other. I received a major life healing for both the night I was taught to say and believe, "It is a great, good thing to be me, because I have You for my God." Do you see the beauty of how they fit together? Jesus is the Father's brilliant "Master stroke" to the identity questions that haunt us: "Who am I?"; "Who are You?" By sending His Son, who is the express Image of His person, to us as *one* of us, our Father is able to reveal exactly what He is like and what it is like to be ourselves as un-fallen human beings (Hebrews 1:3). If you want to know what you're really like deep down as a New Creation, look to Jesus. If you want to know what your Father is really like up in heaven, look to Jesus. Jesus restores both images to our spiritual sight. We need to pause and bow in reverence before the wisdom that reveals such great mysteries to us—through the one and only God-Man, Jesus Christ!

I hardly knew anything at all about these things when I was starting out. All I knew was the pain of what I came to call the "father wound"—a place near my heart that just ached and ached whenever either of those two identity questions would rear their ugly heads. I *hated* it! How little I knew and how very little I appreciated it, that the Father had left this pain for me as a wondrous gift. Instead of removing it, He had turned the father wound, inflicted by the enemy's evil intent, into a homing device that would lead me to Him. I personally do not agree with the common thought that there is a *"God-made* void" inside each of us. There is a God void, yes; it can lead us to God, who alone can fill it, yes. But that He made it? No; that's not what the Bible teaches!

In the beginning I came by my father wound, my God void, honestly. So did you. Adam, our first father, wounded all of us when he ate the forbidden fruit. Adam's rebellion separated not only him from God, it separated all of us as well. In spiritually dying he lost that perfect vision of God which he and Eve had so fully enjoyed and the Image of God he carried in his heart became a twisted thing. Now instead of *knowing in his bones* that God loved him perfectly, he became afraid of God and passed the benighted image of "scary-God-who-wants-to-punish-me" on to us all. The Adam wound was my "First Father" wound and I didn't even know it was there; nonetheless, it was working against me, as it does all of us, blocking us from beholding a true Image of the Father who loves us perfectly. At least this was not my fault. The God void is in us because of Adam; it was his sin that created it. If Satan could have had his way, he would have completely disguised it I'm sure, leaving no trace behind of what we had lost. By sheer mercy God has kept our interior sense alive enough to notice that the Biggest Piece of all is missing. Adam traded it in for an apple. The fear of our fallen nature that Adam's wound instills in us and its mending requires putting the blame squarely on Adam, then forgiving him and taking faith-confidence to know that in no way is God blaming us for having a sin nature. He's simply asking us not to walk in it.

God's backup plan for revealing Himself to us is our earthly fathers. They are the ones who are meant to model for us an accurate image of the true Father, who we are born not knowing due to Adam's sin. Through our birth fathers we are intended to discover what unconditional love is like, along with perfect law-giving justice, grace-giving mercy and a host of other heavenly attributes. Fatherhood is a very high calling (Ephesians 3:15). We all fall short no matter how hard we might try. You simply cannot pass on what you have not received. Until we receive the fullness which Adam enjoyed before his fall we will not be able to pass it on to our sons and daughters. But what we can do is our best, then pray, trusting that God will make good use of it. My dad did his best—he was a good man! Even so, I did not bond with him, but lived in fear of his disapprobation and his hand at punishment. The "Birth Father" wound can also become infected by our own unloving or rebellious reactions, which was certainly the case with me. As I wrote earlier, this wound was mended as I became able to repent of my rebellion against my father, forgiving him from the heart and fully accepting myself as his son.

Then there are the "Father in God" wounds that come our way by religious leaders or others in divinely appointed positions of authority. How many different kinds of father wounds there are! One of this kind came when I was in the sixth grade. I had been sent to the principal's office, though not because I was misbehaving—I was a Doo Bee remember? It was a perk, something like time off for good behavior. I would "watch over" the office while the principal was out. On this particular day, he left the radio playing and there happened to be a hellfire and damnation preacher who was just ripping it up. He thundered that God hated people who drank alcohol so much that even though you had lived for God all your life and never touched a drop of liquor, if you got curious and took a sip, dying with it on your lips, you would go straight to hell. I didn't know any better than to believe him—he was a man of God!

Unfortunately for me, instead of scaring the devil *out* of me, it scared the devil *into* me. From that point on I was running from God! Many, many years later Jesus healed this memory; I saw Him in my mind's eye walk into that office and look kindly at me trembling in fear. He then crossed over to the radio and turned it off. I realized that the "frightened child" still in me didn't feel like he had the authority to stop listening to what the man of God was saying. Jesus' actions showed me that the message hadn't come from Him. We call this kind of mending the "healing of memories." Jesus has many ways of healing a traumatic memory, but it is always on the basis of revealing a greater truth—something from heaven's perspective that we could not see during the crisis—and by getting our heart to believe this greater truth instead of the half-truths or outright lies sown by the enemy. "Father in God" wounds are healed as we forgive those who misrepresented, albeit almost always unintentionally, the true Father to us and lift our eyes of faith to embrace what the "Heavenly Man," Jesus Christ, represents to us of the invisible God (Colossians 1:15).

Nastiest of all is the "Father Imposter" wound which the enemy personally inflicts. You need not have had an occult encounter with the kingdom of darkness as I did to get this one. Jesus said to the *religious* people of His day, "You are of your father the devil...he is a liar and the father of lies" (John 8:44). This father of lies works with the miry clay of our sin nature to "un-make" us according to the pattern of his own demented image. An imposter to the core, he counterfeits real spiritual authority and readily works through false religions and religious spirits to distort the True Image of our All Loving Father. Merely being a Christian or being in church is no guarantee he won't twist your idea of Father God into something that doesn't align with Jesus Christ. Just remember that Jesus and the Father are One (John 10:30). This wound took a long time and much study and prayer to mend, though there was a significant breakthrough that came my way in seminary.

The breakthrough happened near the end of final term senior year. I had some extra time so I was pursuing the Lord by reading an unassigned book, Watchman Nee's *Normal Christian Life*. I lingered over the remark he made about what the Blood of Jesus means to the Father in terms of our acceptance: "The Blood has satisfied God; it must satisfy us also."[6] For some reason that spoke to me and I stopped to reflect on it. From out of nowhere I had the uncanny sense of an unaccustomed Presence drawing near. By now I was somewhat adapted to the Lord Jesus coming and going and the Spirit always remaining, but this was different. This was the Father, and He was very close!

As I waited with bated breath, His words came into my mind. *Son, I have watched you trying so hard to trust and obey Me.* This had been my daily practice from the beginning: "Father, what would you like me to do next?" Since meeting Jesus, there had never been a day when I wasn't pressing in. *I see how cast down you get whenever you lose My peace.* Losing peace is a sign of not fully trusting the Lord or actually following the Spirit. Losing peace always struck fear into me. *You think you might be losing My good grace, that I will turn from you.* That's exactly what I feared! *I want you to know that it's not like that at all. I AM perfect love. What you mistake for a loss of grace is Me awakening you to your need to return. It is My goodness leading you to repentance. I will NEVER forsake you.*

By then I felt so surrounded by love that I dissolved into tears. And I thought: "What have I been living by until now? 'Trust and obey' doesn't go deep enough! I have to make sure I hold fast to *this Image* in my heart. *Everything* depends upon it." I prayed for God to cast down all false images of Himself in my heart just as He had once cast down Dagon from before the ark when it was brought into the Philistine temple. I then began

---

[6] Watchman nee, *The Normal Christian Life* (Wheaton, Illinois: Tyndale House Publishers, Inc., 1957), p. 20.

what has become a lifelong practice of checking to make sure that every morning my heart fully believes the great truths of the Father's perfect love and mercy for me *in every moment*. If there is the slightest shadow of doubt I seek to deal with it. I heartily recommend you do the same—He's your Father too! What you believe about Him in your heart of hearts will make or break your day. Applying my effort to clearing His Image has been the single most important healing process of my Christian life. I need to emphasize that this is not about seeking a *feeling*. I can recall feeling His love only rarely, but I have learned to access the pleasure of fully believing the truth about His love for me. It *always* feels good when you believe Truth from the heart. I am not "hooked on a feeling" like B.J. Thomas's song, but I am hooked on the believing which brings such delightful feelings.

The Occult Legacy (7)

There is an operational side of the kingdom of darkness which we can identify as the occult realm. Not to be able to identify or recognize it can be as dangerous for healthy living as walking through a minefield blindfolded, something I learned the hard way. The Bible was there for me to read and take warning, but I never did. Had I been wise, I would have learned from scripture that some of God's most stringent warnings have to do with avoiding the occult at all costs, even at the pain of death. There are four areas of the occult identified by scripture: worship of false gods (idolatry, false religions), forbidden knowledge of the future (astrology, prognostication), forbidden contact with the dead (séances, mediums), and forbidden access to spiritual power (witchcraft, sorcery). Mercifully, under the New Covenant there is far more grace given to us than there was under the Old Covenant. Unlike ancient Israel we can repent and be forgiven for any sin, even sins of the occult. Additionally we are only called to put the sin to death *in ourselves,* not the occult practitioner! Grace, however, does not change the reality of how deadly and dangerous the occult realm remains for unsuspecting souls who trespass upon its boundaries.

I chronicled for you step-by-step in Part One how I trespassed into the occult, never realizing that it was evil and that it meant me evil, until I was completely snared by it. Even then I was bound by such deception that I continued to believe that the god I had encountered was the true God, and it was only *me* that was evil. From my limited point of view that's a major-league deception, but even what may seem like slight transgressions into this realm can leave a person bound up with confusion, fear and guilt—opening doors for the enemy to bring the curse of the law, the consequence of our disobedience. Freedom and healing come first through recognition and repentance, putting every point of contact with occult practices and beliefs under the Blood of Christ for cleansing, and resolutely turning away from any future involvement, even to the point of burning articles or books you may possess. At Ephesus, when the new believers repented of practicing sorcery, they burned books valued at several million dollars, but the value of being set free from the occult was undoubtedly far greater (Acts 19:18-19). Both June and I went over our past with a fine tooth comb looking for (and finding) points of occult contact to repent of and things in our house that needed to be destroyed, like the Smerf figurines.

I definitely wanted my freedom, but there were things that couldn't easily go under repentance or into the fire. I was stalked by a spooky, shadowy side of what seemed like my former pre-Christian self. It was ghostlike, terrifying and very repelling, but I also felt sorry for it because it seemed so pathetic, *so ruined.* I prayed about it and repented for my past in every way I knew how, but it wasn't until seven or eight years into the walk that I finally saw the last of that ethereal stalker. As I recall I spoke directly to it, told it I was sorry for all it had gone through, but that it had to go to Jesus and leave me in peace *in the Name of Jesus*. I have no clear idea what was really going on in the invisible realm, but whatever lay behind those apparitions, they ended right then and there. I mention this because for those of you who may be seeking freedom from the occult, you need to know that the path of recovery has general outlines provided by scripture, which any good disciple can help you learn, but there are specific steps only the Holy Spirit can show you.

Far more difficult to shake off were two nightmarish legacies from my Night of Terror: the glimpse of the real hell that I had seen; and the message of eternal damnation that I had heard. In my mind I knew that these were things of the past and that they had been exposed as lies from the very first night of my rescue. I was not going to the real hell, nor would the true God ever condemn me—thanks to what Jesus had done and the faith in Him I had been fortunate enough to receive. That should have settled it, but it didn't.

Ideas are held in the mind, but *images* are held in the heart. The things I had experienced were now images rooted in me. Images carry far more spiritual power, which is why the images we have of God and of ourselves *in our heart of hearts* determines the whole course of our lives (Proverbs 4:23; 23:7). We must understand this principle: The Lord has chosen to dwell in our hearts, not our brains. He wants to be where the action is, especially when it comes to cleaning house.

Due to movements of my heart in prayer, I could tell that the Holy Spirit was working with me on these two legacies from the past. A horse that wants to run free often requires a lot of restraint. My heart was bucking and kicking against what was riding me—it definitely didn't like those two images from my Night of Terror. Sometimes there's nothing more to do than cry out loud to God, weep, repent, renounce lies, confess truth—and learn to wait *in hope* upon the Lord. Waiting means hoping; hoping means waiting (Romans 8:24-25). I gave up on waiting. I had so much pain from that protracted occult experience that I became very angry with God for allowing it to happen in the first place and for not removing the pain quick enough to suit me. The only thing I will say in my defense is that this anger didn't arise until I was eleven or twelve years into my walk with God. That's a fair bit of waiting. I was trying to be Job-like in patience; unfortunately I also became Job-like in anger.

Calling it anger isn't quite fair. It was rage. Three signs of occult damage are very high levels of guilt, fear and anger. I had all three signs and all three were intricately bound up with the events of my Night of Terror. I understood that it was my own freewill decisions that had gotten me into that mess and that God had to preserve my freedom of will, but wasn't there something He could have done? Couldn't He have intervened? Did I really have to be dragged down that far? There's no point to these *why* questions, or rather, no point in being stymied by such "cross" interrogations of God for two reasons: God never, ever makes a mistake; and God doesn't usually explain His reasons, especially when we are in a demanding mood. He waits when He sees we are unteachable. Ask Pilate. Or Herod. My granddaughter threw a tantrum on me once when she was three. I just smiled inwardly and waited; time was on my side. It took too much effort for her to maintain her "strategy" for long, and once it passed we set about doing the very thing she had first refused. Because I love her, I hurt for her, but I wasn't about to let her anger rule over her or me. I believe that the Lord is like that with us.

By my calculations, my tantrum lasted at least two years, maybe three. That I didn't get mad at God sooner was really a testimony to how afraid I was of Him. Even so, I didn't want to be angry at all and was trying every way I knew how to get free of my bitterness. Have you noticed that when you are carrying an angry grudge against someone, it seems like everything they do just sets you off? I would go to Him almost every night when I was in the thick of this season of anger and say things like, "Father, I'm so upset about what You allowed to happen today, but I don't want to be angry with You about it." *It's too late, son. You already are. Come, let me have it.* And I would. I would really let Him have it!

One time I shouted so much before releasing the pain to Him in prayer and resubmitting to His leadership over me that I ended up hoarse the next day. All the women on staff at Christ Church made such a fuss over me that I started feeling guilty. They thought I had laryngitis and was bravely "suffering for Jesus." I looked up to the Lord—we were patched up by then—and shared a good laugh. If they only knew; I didn't tell them though! They would have tried to help me and I sensed that this was something that could only be worked out between God and me directly. The simple truth is that if I had gone to a prayer partner or a counselor every time I had an emotional problem from the past, I would have worn out every Christian in Georgia. I was willing to take the hardest things to anyone who was halfway equipped and willing, but I knew that I had to do most of the mountain moving myself.

I may be making light of this season in my life, but it really was a time of very intense anguish. I carried such a knot of emotional pain in my right side just below the ribs that I would gladly have cut it out with a knife, if only it were a true physical pain. After everyone was in bed I would get in my car and seek out secluded spots where I could cry and rage, then release whatever had come up to God on the strength of believing Roman 8:28 over it all: "For the sake of Your redemptive purposes I accept even this..." I had a very real sense that the Holy Spirit was bringing up one broken piece of the past after another and helping me give it to God by this means. Like a fisherman of the soul, He was using events in the present to hook into things of my past that I had pushed down below conscious level. I tried in every way to cooperate with that process, but it was very taxing and tedious.

Eventually, even more healing from the occult damage came through three major moments of ministry. First, I finally identified "death and the grave" as the spirit that came upon me when the real hell almost swallowed me in actual death. Naming it brought the necessary conviction, and I commanded it to leave. This was something I had tried to do a few years earlier while still in seminary, but with no success. This time that deep-seated fear was gone. Second, during this same time in the mid-90s, I was prayed over for at least two hours of intense ministry in the Spirit at a local church—this went a long way towards mending that place in me which still held a terror of being cast into hell again. While that was taking place the Lord showed me that I myself could never make those same mistakes again, now that I knew Him. *It is a new day* reverberated in my mind. A few years later a pastor broke the curse of what I had "heard" as my sentence of final judgment and eternal damnation. That put the icing on the cake.

The thing that ended my anger with God came to me from "out of the blue." I had been looking to repentance, to prayer, to ministries and deliverance. All of this had been moving a mountain of brokenness out of me one anger session at a time, mainly by believing the promise of Romans 8:28 over everything that came up. I reached the point where my heart just wasn't into being angry with God. I could finally see that He truly was innocent, that the occult truly is so evil that I was fortunate to have survived at all and that God was now truly working everything for good as a love-gift to me. Even so, I couldn't stop being angry; it puzzled and shamed me. He certainly deserved to be better treated—especially by me, the one He had rescued from hell. I remember repeatedly asking Him: How could this pattern be broken? That's when the Holy Spirit revealed Jesus to me in a totally unexpected way.

Over a period of two nights I went into our garage and held a crucifix, staring at it and meditating on it until I could gain entrance into *His* sufferings. Paul had prayed in Philippians that he might know Him by somehow sharing in His sufferings. Now that prayer had become my prayer too. Slowly, I began to see that my sufferings—as great as they seemed to me—were still small compared to what He suffered just for me. He suffered the pain of my brokenness and sin, having them placed upon Himself. He suffered the foulness of being made one with my sins. He suffered the wrath and the punishment that I will never know for every one of those sins. He suffers with the Father who grieves over how my sins have caused me so much grief. He suffers with the Holy Spirit who groans and travails within me as He helps me bring my sins to God for cleansing. Here was the shocking revelation—Jesus has suffered far more for my life than I ever had or ever could! And He has suffered like that *for everyone!*

If only my words could convey the majesty of that blazing revelation, or the magnitude of the suffering that the Father, Son and Holy Spirit have gone through for each one of us and with each one of us! By the second night all of my suffering was swallowed up by the grace of letting it give me entry into His suffering. Who can possibly say enough or praise Him as He deserves? The hot flame of indignation over the portion of suffering I had been allowed to experience at long last flickered out. Now I was actually grateful for what I had been through for the sake of what it was revealing to me about my God!

This breakthrough was far more than just being healed of anger; this was a whole new level of love and esteem for the Lord. Paul says that it is only by much suffering that we enter the Kingdom of God. We should listen to Paul. This is the same man who told us that he was willing to cast everything into the fire for the sake of knowing Jesus "in the fellowship of His sufferings" (Philippians 3:10 WEB). I am so glad Paul wrote that! It brought unspeakable consolation to me at that time and has pointed the way for using all kinds of negative events and setbacks as a window into seeing what Jesus is willing to go through for us. With this surrendering of my complaint against

God, with this final acceptance of my life as it had been, the sense of lost wholeness was finally restored. I had arrived home on the inside, and at long last I felt like a "normal" human being!

A Never Ending Story

This is as far as I'm going to take you, for now, on this healing journey. The ending I have brought you to is not the end; life has few moments when loose ends seem nicely tied off and nothing else is unraveling at the moment. No, there is actually *too much* left to fit in here, but all of it can wait for another time. My purpose in this narrative has been to carry you along on my journey of descent into hell, rescue, and return to "normal" Christian living. That is the place I came into some years back when I realized that I finally felt like a human being again and that I was "bored" with my story, so fully had my inward sight shifted from my past to His future. There is a stage to being healed where the very thing you didn't want God or anyone else to know, you now want to tell to the world. Beyond that is the stage where you no longer care if you ever tell it again—unless He asks it of you. He asked it of me, and now I have told it, fully believing that this is the season I decided to wait for in the aftermath of Honduras, when the wine of my testimony would reach maturity and could be freely shared at last.

The truth is that our journeys never end; they stretch from here to heaven, where the real adventure finally begins. For now I can only say how grateful I am to have had this opportunity to write to you. It has brought the One my heart loves very close to my side as I laughed and cried my way through these remembrances. I hope it has also brought Him close to you. Have you, perhaps, heard a faint "echo" of His whispering? It would be very much like the Lord to cast His light—light as a feather—upon some dark passage in your life as you have been reading about my own.

Are we really so different? As bizarre as my life has been, is it not in some rudimentary ways but a reflection of your own? You, too, against all odds and beyond all deserving, have been *rescued from hell*. A Great Love has also been pursuing you, laying claim to your heart and fighting for your freedom from the depredations of an unseen enemy. Though that battle took center stage in my life, it is no less real if it has been going on behind the scenes in yours. Whether we realize it or not, all of us who believe in Jesus have a tale to tell of desperate peril and impossible rescue, of unimaginable grace and glorious return!

REFLECTIONS

A Very Disturbing Thought

Perhaps the reason I have never heard a testimony like my own is that people who have been trapped in this deception died while believing they were in hell already—and "awakened" in the real hell, or they are still in it, but are too scared to talk about it just as I was. What if the devil has done something like this to a lot of other people?

Scientists of the Mind Revisited

One of the arguments for the existence of God, oddly enough, is the reality of evil. Not garden variety evil such as our selfish ways and foolish thinking—these we all readily accept as commonplace and comprehensible. Rather it is the unsettling outbreaks of raw, inexplicable evil, whether it is sadistic torture applied to innocent victims or the inward unrelenting, torture of psychotic breakdowns such as I experienced. Why would we do that to each other or ourselves? You can't take rational people, self-interest (enlightened or otherwise), a strictly materialistic universe, and explain the proliferation of raw evil that fills columns within our newspapers and minds within our mental wards. As we say in Georgia, "You can't get there from here!"

Here is common sense reality: an exquisitely beautiful planet with most new children arriving in nearly pristine, cuddly condition. Look no further. Here is where the sensible view, one held by the vast majority of mankind regardless of time or place, sees that there is surely a great, good Creator. We may not know Him, but we know He is good and He left a moral order for us to follow. Conscience is our guide. Admittedly, this sensible view has a hard time explaining real evil—how did *that* enter the picture? Did the Creator mess up? Is there something *wrong* with God? Did *we* do it? Despite these questions, the obvious and sensible explanation to all of the beauty and order that surrounds and sustains us is that there is a Creator.

If you don't take the sensible view you would have to successfully explain away the existence of conscience—God's homing beacon—and then silence your own. That done, you would still have to believe against unthinkable mathematical probabilities that all of nature and the universe came about on its own. If you can take that leap of faith, you're ready to create a world view that eliminates God, but you still can't get there. Not when *there* includes the unspeakable horrors of unbridled evil. It takes one heck of a theory to encompass all the evil inflicted by humanity and upon humanity without calling in the devil from off stage to rescue the plot line, like the *Deus ex Machina* device of ancient literature. In a strictly material world how do you get in-human and un-human from merely human? *How can man explain man?* It can't be done. Yet this is the great philosophical project of the scientists of the mind.

I think my story, for those who give it credence, would shatter the vain attempt to understand psychology without any reference to spiritual realities. How do you dredge up from the depths of human psyche the ability and power to confine yourself in a fully realized version of hell and then hold that delusion in place for ten years with unbroken precision? I didn't even have the ability to clap in time with music for more than halfway through a song, much less hold two thoughts in place for a day. How do you explain the stunning, utterly transcendent encounters with not one but *two* divine beings, who were radically different from each other, and which produced in me *each time* a radically transformed manner of living, thinking, imagining and desiring?

This was not merely inward experience and imagining—*everyone* who knew me saw the lifestyle changes that took place following each encounter. These two changes came naturally, spontaneously and with lasting effect. I didn't have to say, "Hey, I'm a hippie pantheist," or, "Do you know I'm a Christian now?" The changes were obvious at every level, and yet I was never in any conscious way trying to produce them. None of these changes were forced; they were the logical, inevitable and immediate outcomes of the all-encompassing encounters I had with these two supernatural beings and of the world view transformations those encounters initiated.

Perhaps you are willing to believe that I encountered supernatural beings. I certainly met one gentleman who was not. This chance meeting took place within the first year of my liberation from hell and conversion to Christianity. I was still working at Timberworks at the time, when a very distinguished man entered my shop to talk about possible woodwork. I steered the conversation towards spiritual things and salted in just a tiny bit of my testimony to see if he would take the bait. Did he ever! It turned out he was a psychiatrist, working on a book about schizophrenia! *Really? That was my diagnosis—paranoid schizophrenia—when I was at Duke's Meyer Ward.* Naturally, he knew the place with professional respect.

He began very excitedly explaining *his theories* about schizophrenia to me. I asked if he had a clinical interest in hearing what it was like *on the inside* from someone who was now completely free of the delusion. He didn't want his theory-explaining entirely set aside, but politely agreed to listen. I quickly launched into the madness, then I brought it around to the vision of Jesus on the throne of grace, and finally to having seven demons cast out of me by my friend Eddy. I got more excited as I talked—here was someone from the psychiatric community who was actually trying to understand and help people like I had once been. Surely, this was a divine appointment!

I saw this as a chance for me to seed into his benevolent work, some actual hard facts that might help *them*—the people still in torment. I held a key to the mystery—the inside story of one person's experience and recovery from a terribly baffling mental illness. I could tell him what works and what doesn't work, as applied to schizophrenia. He wanted none of it and began to shut down. He had obviously heard enough and didn't want more. Nothing I was telling him fit into his nice *theories*, and his book was already well underway. He told me that the doctors at Duke had obviously diagnosed me incorrectly; otherwise I couldn't be this sane. But I don't think he thought I was sane, not after mentioning the demons coming out of me! He said he was sorry they had put a wrong label on me and was gone. I never found out why he had stopped by Timberworks in the first place.

This leaves me wondering how people who don't believe in the existence of demons can help others get free of them. I'm going to make a sweeping statement: Behind all sickness, behind all disease, behind all mental disorders, behind all addictions, behind all character defects are structures of demonic oppression. Demons are real! St. Paul warns us that "We do not wrestle against flesh and blood [these are not merely human issues], but against the rulers, against the authorities, against the cosmic powers over this present darkness, against the spiritual forces of evil in the heavenly places" (Ephesians 6:12). That's heaven's perspective on our problem.

Along with the above consideration, I'm prepared to make another statement just as sweeping: Inside all sickness, inside all disease, inside all mental disorders, inside all addictions, inside all character defects are people who desperately want God to find them and free them. The God void is real. It has been observed that "the young man who rings the bell at the brothel is unconsciously looking for God."[7] So is the man looking for a way out of the asylum. God, the One who should know, says that He put eternity into *every* heart (Ecclesiastes 3:11). Every last one of us, no matter what our proud boasting

---

[7] Bruce Marshall, *The World, the Flesh and Father Smith* (Boston, MA: Houghton Mifflin Company, 1945), p. 108. Often mistakenly attributed to G. K. Chesterton.

may be, knows deep inside that the God connection is broken and that it needs to be fixed. The simple truth is that we were created for God, and as Augustine famously observed, our hearts are going to stay restless until they find their rightful home in Him.

I have no doubt that the scientists of the mind are humane and well-intentioned. Those that I have met with few exceptions, most notably "The Rock," have been men and women of obvious compassion, subtle and well-trained understanding and ingenious insight. They have chosen to labor in a very difficult field that most ordinary people shy away from: the emotionally and mentally broken. Even so, I believe that they are unwittingly laboring against an insurmountable handicap. They would seek to make people whole without bringing them to God.

On the human level, they have yet to develop a unified theory of personhood or personality. The general public seemed to have had great interest in the beginning when the "new science" produced its early masters. Freud, Jung and Adler were practically household names. Perhaps it seemed then that the psychiatrist would subsume the role of priest as healer and psychiatry that of Christianity. A new world was dawning. All was about to be explained. Where religion had failed in the attempt, man would explain man to man. That was one hundred years ago. The world at large is no longer looking in this direction for either revelation or for guidance. Now they are mostly looking for pills. Pills are helpful, but they cannot make people whole. For that their Maker is required.

The real handicap is at the spiritual level. It takes two main forms. The first is the difficulty of mending people whose main problem is that they do not have the relationship with God that they need and that God desires them to have. This has been lost; it is crying out to be restored, especially among those who most resist acknowledging their need of it. Every one of us has been created to live entirely surrendered to God in full awareness of His love and in full submission to His will. *Nothing less than this constitutes a reasonable cure.* To clear the way for this, the healing agent needs to have spiritual eyes to see both the demonic obstructions and the divine initiatives. Those who would heal our souls are largely blind on both counts.

This blindness would be trouble enough, but there is a larger difficulty to explain, if you are willing to go further with me into a Christian perspective. God, who is the true Healer, surely works through every means available to Him. This we call grace and I have no doubt that it is at work even for the benefit of those psychiatrists and patients who reject the Grace Giver. However, here's the rub: God may not be nearly as interested in giving short-term success to psychiatrists or to their patients as He is in bringing both of them to His salvation through a true knowledge of Himself. The stakes are too high. Every baleful condition I mentioned earlier—illness, disease, mental disorder, addictions, character defects—from a Christian point of view, may be His sovereign means for bringing to His salvation *a soul who is running from Him.* The healer is meant to recognize this work of God and cooperate with it.

I am an obvious case in point. At a crucial period the mental wards kept me from taking my life and I am very appreciative of that saving work. Maintenance has real value. However, nothing psychiatry attempted ever mended me and ten years of anguish followed for the salient reason that God was intent on revealing Himself to me and I had foolishly shut and barred the door. This was the biggest fact about me in terms of where it had all gone wrong in my life, but I never thought to mention it in counseling—no one ever asked. God was literally using hell on earth as a means of returning me to Himself, but the cure *required* me believing in Him. Was there anything in a psychiatric textbook that could have guessed at the secret purpose of God, working *through* my delusion? Please don't misunderstand. I certainly don't believe that I was being crushed by God. He loves me and never wanted me to fall so far from grace.

These were my own foolish choices, but He was using the painful consequence of my sins, the delusion of hell, in a redemptive way for which I am now incredibly grateful.

Have we not heard that God opposes the proud? He opposed me in my pride-filled attempt to become whole without Him. He opposed the pride of a profession which tried to help me become whole without leading me to the One who alone could heal me. He *has* to oppose us. If He didn't I would have been lost to Him and to myself *forever*. Since God loves everyone equally, let's extend this logically. The great obstacle psychiatry faces is the foolishness of seeking to bring wholeness to humanity while leaving God out; the great Resister of the longed-for success may be *at times* the very God it excludes. For our own sake God has to resist our foolish efforts to shut Him out of our lives.

A Law Abiding Citizen in Hell

Ironically, even though I saw myself as a horrible sinner rejected by my god and justly punished by being damned to hell forever, I was living a more morally upright life than many born-again Christians I have since met. How could this be?

Consider these contrasts: I was a former drug abuser, a college dropout, a society dropout, a political radical and a rejecter of Christian revelation with nothing to live for. I didn't even have God to fear, since I believed myself to have been utterly abandoned by Him. In addition I was filled with rage, terror, fear, abject despair, utter hopelessness, self-hatred, extreme bitterness, inward cursing, wild and crazy thoughts, a seething cauldron of sexual fantasy and profound impulses to violence—all on a 24/7 basis. I was mentally deranged by the deception, insane by any reasonable standard.

Ironically, I was also a faithful husband, devoted father, honest businessman, fair employer and beginning to be a community leader: in short, a model citizen. I had many friends. As manager of a small factory my bankers said they trusted me more than the man I was working for. Later, our own business also had a very good name in the community. One family member often said that I had been a better Christian *before* my conversion, than afterwards, when I started preaching to her.

It was hell on the inside; good citizen on the outside! There is no doubt in my mind that I would have ended up in the real hell if Jesus hadn't rescued me, even from my "model" life! Nevertheless, I apparently had something going for me that many *normal* people fail to connect with, even people who know the true God as their Savior and presumed Lord. What was it? The answers may surprise you. I only saw them when I began writing this book.

Here is what I can see that I had going for me: I thought my life was over so I had completely given up all my selfish and self-centered dreams. All thought of trying to get pleasure, fortune, fame, or power out of life had died with me in hell. None of that would change hell one iota, so I had no interest in those foolish goals. I was purged *by hell* of a lot of the selfish desires that fuel so much depraved behavior, such as my own earlier misguided pursuits. This was a great advantage!

I was therefore absolutely convinced that I couldn't improve myself or my position. I couldn't change myself into a better version, so I stopped trying altogether; ironically, this too was a blessing. God can work on what we take our hands off of, but He won't pry things out of our fingers. It doesn't seem to matter if we don't specifically give it to Him, just as long as He sees that we have truly let it go. It's called grace and He gives it out impartially to all. God, without my knowing or my conscious cooperation, began working all kinds of good changes into me once I quit working on myself. This was grace working on me.

I couldn't improve myself or my condition (both were hopeless), but I was extremely aware that I could make everything and anything a lot worse. I had been thoroughly schooled by the enemy in the law of sowing and reaping as one aspect of the way hell operated. In actual reality, this *is* how the universe operates, once you add in the graced-based interventions of God. There really is a law of sowing and reaping—it is the law that governs all laws—and there really is a God who rewards everyone according to their deeds. Without realizing it I had recovered a modicum of respect for the true God by learning to respect this one great law of His.

Being very aware that everything I did had a consequence in hell, I became determined to make sure that I kept the law of retribution from working against me. I had no concept that the law of sowing and reaping could actually work *for* me. Still, *this one understanding* was enough to make me diligent to restrain all the evil that was inside of me as much as I possibly could. I didn't want to let any of the interior hell that was in me get out; that would inevitably lead to the breaking of Rule #2: Don't do anything that would land me back in Cherry Hospital or in jail. I *couldn't* let myself act loony or lawless. Do you know that you have that kind of power over yourself? Everyone does. God has given the power to choose between life and death to each one of us (Deuteronomy 30-19).

This made me a very devoted *law keeper*. Keeping the law will not save you—you need faith in Jesus for that; it cannot heal you of hell inside you—you need to learn how to trust, to forgive and to release issues to God for that. It cannot help you live with natural grace, childlike and free—you need a life in the Spirit for that. It didn't do any of these things for me. I would have loved if it could have. But I wasn't embracing the law in the form of my Rules 1-4 in the hope that it would accomplish any of those desirable goals, so I never gave up on what the law actually could do for me. In Romans, Paul says that the law was given as a restraint upon sin. You can put a huge period right at the end of that! This is why I loved the law then and still do. My "laws" were there to keep me from disaster. For me there was no God, but there was enlightened self-interest. Being devoted to the law, being an industrious law keeper, kept me out of a lot of trouble! What I didn't know and couldn't notice was that law keeping actually allowed the true God to secretly be growing a good life all around me since He is the Rewarder of those who *do* good. By keeping my laws I was *doing* good, not evil.

To sum it up I had both the Biblical fear of God and a love for the law, although in debased forms. I didn't know or believe in the true God, and I didn't believe the Bible for other laws, but I *totally* respected the law of sowing and reaping. That was enough to make me a good citizen, keep me out of all kinds of further trouble, and gain some of the blessings that are promised to anyone with enough godly fear to be a law keeper. As a pastor it seems to me that many Christians make the mistake of trying to be law-abiding in order to gain God's approval and then fall into the trap of thinking God can't be very pleased with them because they aren't perfect at keeping the law. Others seem to think that God's grace means that the law no longer matters, and therefore they live with apparent disregard for the law of sowing and reaping. Either way it's a disaster!

For me the ultimate irony is that I was running the race hogtied with hell on the inside of me and hell surrounding me, but as it turns out *I was running in God's direction!*

HEALING STREAMS MINISTRY

Healing Streams is a ministry of liberation and transformation founded by Steve Evans and his first wife, June, the year before she died. It is now being carried on by Steve and Eunice Evans. Through Biblical teaching we seek to help people find freedom from the negative emotions that rob inner peace and damage health. Our main healing lessons form a 24 part series, *Matters of the Heart*, which can be accessed for free through our website as individual, downloadable teachings in PDF and MP3 formats or viewed on our Youtube channel. In addition to our presence on the web, we host "live" weekday and weekend seminars in beautiful Savannah, Georgia.

Contact us at
info@healingstreamsusa.org
Visit us on the web at
www.healingstreamsusa.org
www.youtube.com/healingstreamsusa
www.facebook.com/healingstreamsusa

Healing Streams Ministry is a division of Forerunner Ministries, Inc., a 501(c)3 nonprofit corporation (Federal Tax ID# 030557651).

BOOKS FROM FORERUNNER

If you enjoyed *Rescued from Hell*, consider purchasing copies for friends at www.createspace.com/3785359 and keep exploring the spiritual life through these other insightful books by Steve Evans, available at Amazon.com, Healingstreamsusa.org or Alibris.com.

Matters of the Heart is a 24 lesson workbook designed to guide believers through the basic understandings necessary for releasing emotional damage from the past and gaining a grace-based restoration to wholeness. Each chapter is filled with "tools" for practical application. 276 pages. Paperback: $20.00.

The Missing Peace includes all of the 24 lessons of the *Matters of the Heart* teaching series, but without the workbook's other material, focusing instead on the stream of scriptural revelation that will show you how to bring your heart to God and receive His Heart for you in return. 194 pages. Paperback: $15.00.

An Illustrated Guide to the Spiritual Life captures in living color, with playful insights, the otherwise elusive, invisible realities of our life in God. These illustrations are intended for the general reader as well as being a companion booklet to *The Missing Peace*. 56 pages. Paperback: $10.00.

Good Grief is not for everyone, but for those who despite their pain have "set their hearts on pilgrimage," determined to make it to the other side of the Valley of Tears, allowing sorrow that is *rightly* carried to mend their hearts and guide their lives toward God's new beginning. 70 pages. Paperback: $7.00.

Made in the USA
Charleston, SC
18 October 2012